THE CONFIDENT PARENT'S GUIDE TO RAISING A HAPPY, HEALTHY & SUCCESSFUL CHILD

EMMA GRANT

NOTEBOOK
PUBLISHING

First published in the United Kingdom in 2019 by Notebook Publishing,
20–22 Wenlock Road, London, N1 7GU.
www.notebookpublishing.com

ISBN: 9781913206260

Typeset by Notebook Publishing.

I would like to thank my husband, Paul, along with my two children, Holly and Dylan, for always, supporting, encouraging and believing in me to follow my dreams all these years.

I would also like to thank my late Nan Marion for being my inspiration.

My Mum and Dad for teaching me lessons no one else could.

And to those non biological Mother and Father figures and in-laws who have supported me, too.

CONTENTS

PRAISE FOR EMMA GRANT

Reading your books has been a joy. You are well versed, well spoken, clearly knowledgeable on your topic, and crazy inspiring. I have not only implemented many of your techniques, but I have been parroting you to my boys for months. 'Can't is just can with a T for try!' But seriously, you have a wonderful book here. I will be recommending it like crazy the minute it hits the shelves!

You actually inspired me to make a schedule and put it on the wall for my two younger ones to help them with keeping time with the day and what is expected. They love it! No more 'what are we doing today, mom?' They feel more in control and informed. So, thanks! I happened to agree with all of your points and your views, notably, I am the mother of 7 children, 6 of them boys, and I found your work to be spot on, inspiring, and a helpful refresher. For new parents it will be invaluable, for more experienced parents it can help get them back on track when we tend to wander off into auto parenting (I read the second book). I have to say, I loved your books! Your content is excellent, solid and is delivered with a wonderful tone that is relatable and engaging, I love this book! I hope it does well; so many parents would benefit from it. From one mom to another, well done! You have earned my respect and a good helping of awe.

—*Marni Macrae*
Mum to Edain, Sarah, Joe, Toby, Noah, Dominic, and the rascal Lucas

The book is really great. Love the *Stick to your Guns* section!

I Love how the middle section of the book has a real emphasis on the parent and their needs and lovely inclusion of space for U time.

Honestly overall it's brilliant and I cannot wait to purchase a copy. Please let me know when it is out so I can tell all the parents at my Church, friends and mother and toddler group! Thank you for allowing me the opportunity to read the book, it has been a privilege.

—Katherine Carreira Mum to Jorge and José

Our three children spent many years with this fantastic couple, who have played such a big part in our lives.

Our son was nine months old when I returned to work. Emma and Paul helped with every aspect of his development. I could work daily knowing that he was in safe hands and enjoying himself with the various activities that took place.

Our daughter went every morning and after school. Then our third child started two years ago. All three children enjoyed socialising with all the other children, and enjoyed all the home-cooked meals.

We are truly grateful for everything they have done for us and will always remain good friends; in fact, they are now godparents to our three children and classed as our best friends.

Thank you.

—Lisa & Ian Griffiths, Mum & Dad to Megan, Jack & Joshua

Our daughter Laila was so happy every day she spent with Emma and Paul, she always left with a massive smile and enjoyed telling us about her day on the way home.

While Laila was with Emma and Paul I felt that her development came on leaps and bounds and her interactions with others became so good.

Emma and Paul were extremely helpful when it came to things like potty training as Laila had just started when she was with Emma and Paul.

We're really grateful for the time Laila had with Emma and Paul right up to the last day when we moved house. We were all sad to say goodbye especially Laila, she made lots of friends and misses them till this day.

Thank you for everything you guys did with Laila and for Laila, we really appreciate it. Thank you, Emma.

—*Ben and Jade Shahab, Laila's mum and dad*

I cannot thank you Emma and Paul enough for the amazing care you have taken of Jac, I always felt happy to leave my 'baby' with you. During my son's time with Emma, he grew in confidence and ability, which I am sure Emma and Paul directly contributed to. Emma has helped my son to use the toilet and put his shoes and coat on. His shyness disappeared and was replaced by enthusiasm to mix with others. His independence has grown a great deal because of his time with Emma and Paul, he talks fondly of them both and his time in their home or out at various fun venues. Occasions are marked by fun, creative and educational activities. He loves to present us with things made at Emma's for Mother's Day, Father's Day, Easter or Christmas. The disco at Christmas was a particular treat and seeing the children having so much fun was touching and memorable. The children in Emma and Pauls care are looked after in a nurturing, consistent and calm environment in which they are encouraged to express themselves through play and creative activity. My son uses role play freely since his time with Emma and as a result is able to play well with his sister at home and has developed close friendships with his peers. It has been a pleasure to have someone who has such child centred ideals, look after my child whilst I am in work. Emma has shown on countless occasions that she genuinely loves children and treats them all as special, unique individuals. You have helped me out as a friend on numerous occasions and I am so very, very grateful for your kindness. It is so reassuring to be able to trust someone totally with your child and know they are in great hands. I would recommend Emma to anyone.

—*Lisa Cordery-Bruce (midwife, school nurse) and Mum to Jac & Bethan*

Emma and Paul have been looking after my 4 children for nearly 7 years. My children settled in instantly with them when they were babies. They are a lovely couple and their home is a very welcoming environment - they treat all the children they look after as their own. They have been a great help with potty training and with their many years of experience it didn't take long for my children to grasp it which made life so much easier for me. Time is made for reading stories and singing songs which has helped immensely with their speech and vocabulary. My children have enjoyed many trips to the farm and playcentres with Emma, Paul and their family. My children have also gained friendships with the other children they look after. Emma and Paul are highly professional and are very passionate about what they do. They have been an absolute god send to me and I don't know what I would have done without them. I have been able to go to work and have no worries about my children as I know they are looked after fantastically! Emma & Paul are the best childminders ever.

—*Gemma Summers Mum to Jasmine, lily, Ruby & Joel*

I met Emma during a paediatric first aid training course. At this time, I was unaware I was pregnant with my second child, my daughter. I followed Emma on social media over the years and kept in contact. When it was time for me to find childcare, I was reluctant to use private day care and got in contact with Emma. She was very friendly, reassuring and welcoming.

My daughter took a while to settle due to only attending 1 day a week. Emma was very patient, trying to keep similarities from home to allow my daughter to feel safe. She kept me up to date with photographs and sending me messages on how she was doing. This gave me reassurance as I felt guilty leaving her. However, a few months in and my daughter has gained so much confidence and become more independent.

Emma is very passionate about her work and we always have long conversations due to parenting and our professions. I am very lucky to have met Emma on the course a few years ago.

—*Danielle Nealon, Mum to Raya*

My daughter Tegan has been with Happy Childcare for two years now. My daughter was in two nurseries prior to starting with Happy Childcare and she was happy in them but she never really settled. Within two weeks of starting with Emma and Paul my daughter was noticeably happier and had a surge in confidence. I know Tegan is so happy being there with them daily and every day she has learnt something new and is excited to tell me about it when I pick her up. She has made many friends there and looks forward to going to Happy Childcare to start her day.

From a parent's perspective, there is nobody else I would entrust to look after my daughter. I have been through some personal and financial issues during Tegan's time with Emma and Paul and the support that I received from them is massive. They have been supportive and flexible and I know I can turn to them should I need to. I have recently moved home and even stayed in the same area so Tegan can stay with Emma.

—Rhiannon Thomas, Mum to Tegan

My son Dylan settled in with Emma & Paul very well and is always excited to go to their house and never wants to leave. I'm very happy with Dylan's care, they are such a lovely family. They have also got Dylan to eat vegetables at dinner already after 2 weeks which is a miracle!

—Sam Reed, Mum to Dylan

Paul and Emma looked after my daughter for two years. In those two years she gained another family. We both did. She would come home beaming and full of stories of what they did that day.

She was looked after as she was their own child. I can't thank Paul and Emma enough for all they have done. They are such a kind, caring, welcoming family. Their own children are an absolute credit to them. We were so sad on the last day but have kept close contact with them since.

It was lovely going to work and not having to worry about my child. She was taken to and from school fed home cooked meals and always had great fun doing plenty of activities.

—5* childcare x Lauren Richardson, Mum to Taigah

I have found Emma and Paul to be extremely helpful and nothing is ever too much trouble. They do a variety of activities with the children both inside and outside the home and they go on numerous trips to the park, lakes, parties and of course the wacky. They interact with a lot of other children through toddler groups as well as playing with Emma's own children all of whom are caring polite and wonderful role models. Not only do Emma and Paul look after the children physically but they give them loads of love and affection too. They are well fed throughout the day and any special like they have are catered for. They have done a really good job with potty training Leo. They have got pets but it is excellent opportunity for children who are afraid of them, like my son was, now he has no more bad feelings about dogs we can walk in the park without screaming and crying. I have found Emma and all her family to be exemplary people and I'm so glad that my children had the benefit of her care for the time that they did.

—Katarina Medve, Mum to Leo & Lexi

I'm just writing to say how grateful Neil and I are for your help picking up Nia from school. As you know we were very worried that no childminder would say yes to what would be such a small job to them, and not particularly profitable financially. To us, it was the most important job in the world, making sure that Nia was collected from school, safely, and we are so pleased and impressed that you appreciated our need and agreed to help. To us it shows that you really care for the children, and that it isn't just a job. Nia was unaffected by the change in routine, and that is all credit to you both for making her feel at ease straight away. Each time

Delyth and I arrived at your house to collect Nia we were greeted with the same warm welcome and the delicious smell of home cooking!

—*Julia and Neil Greenwood Mum and Dad to Nia & Delyth*

Emma and Paul have been Trina's childminders for 3 years during this time they have become like an extended family to the two of us and we are going to miss them a lot! They provide healthy, fresh meals for the children in their care and promote healthy eating! They also provide stimulating activities for the children, often based on a child's interests! I would recommend Emma and Paul to anyone!

—*Gemma Strevens, Mum to Katrina*

My daughter has been in childcare with Emma and Paul since she started primary school. She is now in her final year. I will be beyond gutted to not have the peace of mind in the mornings that Emma and Paul have got my child off to school safely without me having to worry about anything. Their family environment is always welcoming, their own children are a credit to them and my daughter idolises them. It's literally a second home, my child is treated as their own child while she is in their care. I can always count on them for help with care out of my days if I'm stuck, they are more than accommodating and so so reliable.

Their rates are fair and it's more than value for money knowing how well they look after my child. You will not be disappointed with this childcare service! 5 star!

—*Adele French, Mum to Tilly*

Emma is a fantastic Childcare provider who looked after my boys who were 4 and 3 years, she is not just a childminder but a caregiver and really looks after your childrens wellbeing, from the food she feeds them to the things she teaches them, you can tell she really cares, Emma also helped me out with potty training and gave me some really helpful tips and support, my boys used to come home really happy and to this day my eldest, who is now almost 6 will still run and give her a hug when he's sees her at the school, he will also say 'I miss Emma and Paul'.

—*Kelly Linsey, Mum to Keegan, Kayle & Kiyah*

Please send me the link to this book after publication; I have a group I would like to share it with. It's amazing! A must-have for every home.

—*Michelle D., a mother and avid reader of parenting books*

INTRODUCTION

'Childhood is a precious time full of magic and mystery. Parenting is full of manic and ambiguity!'

—*Emma Grant*

I STARTED WRITING MY parenting self-help books over a decade ago as a young Mum to a baby and a two-year-old toddler and a Registered Childminder caring for other peoples' children at the same time. I won't lie, it was a stressful start to my parenting journey and to my childcare career!

One laced with many self-doubts and on the job learning and training the hard way. One saviour I had was my love of reading, so in order to get what I believed to be the most important job in the world—parenting and childcare—right, I scoured the book shops for resources to help me do the best job possible for all the children I cared for. I found many books on different subjects but not one that I was really looking for. Hence, the reason why I wrote this book for you.

What I lacked back then was experience and confidence, now, with over sixteen years of experience and confidence later, you hold in your hands the book I wished I could have read back then, with the results of all I now know.

Like me, you will still encounter times of self-doubt and inexperience, but by the end of this book, you will have a newfound confidence in your parenting abilities and a robust, tried and tested routine that works to help you raise happy, healthy, and confident children.

I'm now a qualified hypnotherapist, nutritional therapist, parent coach, registered childcare provider, author, and Mum to two teenagers. What I will say is—we are all happy, healthy, and successful together, and parenting so far has been truly a joyous gift and experience for myself and my husband. So much so, when we reached our forties, he had a vasectomy reversal after eleven years so we could start all over again, I'll keep you posted on our progress... but that's another book in the making!

Here we will keep our focus on the children we already have, and the influence we can have over their lives. But before we can convince our children to do as we want them to, we have to feel confident that what we are asking them to do is the right thing for the right reasons and at the right time. And for that to happen, we need to have a plan we believe in.

The U URSELF Routine that's outlined in this book will help you do just that, and once you start implementing it in your child's life, you'll both enjoy revelling in the results.

Confidence is key, so chapter one will address who is to blame for our lack of parenting confidence today and how to regain that confidence back through self-awareness and keeping up.

In chapter two you will be introduced to the U URSELF Routine and twelve points on when and how to start. Preparation is king when it comes to confidence, so please don't skip this essential part and jump straight into the magic of making it happen. Patience, as you will soon discover, paves the path to success.

But that success all starts with you, which is why U Time, chapter three, starts with time for you. We will explore where your time goes, who cares for you if you don't, minding your own business, and how to dump that guilty rubbish once and for all and make every day special.

Carrying on with the 'Busyness Disease' in chapter four, Us Time, we will be looking at quantity versus quality time and uncover how precious duvet days and us time really are, and the value in making daily individual Us Time for each child. This continues into Recreation and The Power of Play in chapter four where we learn how to grow up childish and how to play properly.

A warning here though, this could unlock your 'jack in the box' and be fun, as we will soon see, only boring people get bored, so get your child ready for a bit of fun and a boogie in chapter five, before bed time, where we will reveal the solutions to sleep success in chapter six.

Hopefully, by chapter seven we will be feeling more confident and ready to make our children feel good in, 'Esteem—Teaching Our Children to be Selfish.' By exploring our children's self-belief, self-image, self-respect, self-confidence, and self-limiting beliefs, we will aim to increase their overall self-esteem. This chapter explores offering games and tools and techniques such as; Affirmations, Playing the As If Game, Three Happy Things, and The Bother Box.'

But don't worry, that will be followed by lashings of love in chapter eight where we discover our true, unconditional, loving bond and how it's never too late to repair that kink in the chain of love that connects us to our children.

If that's not enough food for thought, then the final part of the U URSELF routine in chapter nine, is all about food and the mealtime, mayhem experience. Here we will be digesting our children's nutritional needs and fussy eating, the changes in our food habits, table manners, emotional eating, and swallowing our own advice.

Next, we will be successfully moving on to the only greens we should be insisting our children devour in chapter ten—Learning Fun for Everyone and The Four P's in the Pod.

Finishing off, we will discuss the Seven Steps to Success in chapter eleven;

1. Enthusiasm
2. Aspiration
3. Intention
4. Motivation
5. Decisiveness
6. Failure
7. Resilience

You will find throughout this book certain points reiterated throughout, especially the point I persistently make about acknowledging our children's efforts as much as their achievements, that's because I believe this is key to raising a happy, healthy and successful child and is relevant in all areas of their life, if this is the only thing you take away from reading this book then I will consider the writing of this book a success.

You can also find a small glossary at the end of common terms used throughout the book and a final word in Enjoy the Process and Get in Touch, before we say goodbye.

Your child is a gift. To unwrap the present, let's get started. Are you ready to feel confident?

Who said no? Well, you soon will be!

So grab a notebook (or ideally a journal that you can continue to use after reading this book) and pen as you read, as there will be plenty of opportunities throughout for you to take part in some simple self-reflective exercises. These aren't compulsory, but you'll gain the most benefit from this book if you do complete them. Writing things down excels the reflective learning process.

Let's go!

CHAPTER 1:
CONFIDENCE IS KEY

FOLLOW THE LEADER

As PARENTS, WE ARE our children's leaders.

If we can show them that we are confident in what we are saying or expecting them to do, then they will follow our lead as we proactively guide, teach, support, encourage, and inspire them in the right direction... well, most of the time anyway.

Confidence is the biggest quality all good leaders demonstrate. Everyone wants to be on the team with the most confident leader because they inspire confidence in others, and they take responsibility.

Would you trust a sports coach who didn't feel he could help his team win or a surgeon who didn't feel confident in his abilities to perform an operation on you?

Not only do those leaders need to feel confident in themselves to carry out those roles, but we need to feel confident in them. It's the same with parenting, we need to feel confident in our own parenting abilities for our children to have confidence in us.

Did you ever play 'Follow the Leader' as a child?

Children love that game, and why?

Because children like nothing more than being led and following and copying others, it's how they learn.

This is great news for us parents!

Why then, do so many of us still struggle to feel confident and to lead our children?

IS IT ME OR IS IT MY CHILD?

As parents, we sometimes wonder: Is the problem me or is my child a problem child?

This uncertainty knocks our confidence. Either way, we feel we are failing.

We question ourselves because over the last fifty years, life has changed so dramatically, at such a fast pace. The old ways of doing things have changed, leaving us lost with no proven way forward.

We just don't know anymore what to do for the best as we can't measure ourselves against a norm that no longer exists. Advances in technology, how we interact with others, and the dynamics of the family unit have all changed.

It's difficult to measure how well we are doing as parents. Parenting roles have become strenuous and complex, and we're facing challenges that, traditionally, our grandparents would never have faced.

Despite a lot of positive changes in lifestyles and advancements in technology, life has become harder, not easier for parents. Yes, we now have a dishwasher to save us time, but we are now using that time to do more things. Instead of just relaxing with our families, we find ourselves multitasking everything. Our children do have more opportunities today than ever before, but these all cost more time, money, and energy. This accessibility to everything, worldwide, twenty-four seven, including work, means we no longer have downtime to relax and think straight, or simply to enjoy spending daily, family time together.

IT'S NOT OUR CHILDREN'S FAULT

Juggling everything has become impossible, and somewhere in our effort to do so, we are losing that loving, human connection with our children.

As a result, we can no longer effectively communicate or understand our children or their needs—making them somewhat of an enigma to us like an Alien Species sent to test our patience.

The real story, however, is our children, who love us unconditionally, don't understand us.

They don't know what it is we expect of them or why. Because much of the time, we are not sure either.

And they have no way of articulating that to us.

They don't understand how things affect our emotions such as tiredness, sadness, stress, anxiety, being overworked and underpaid, or the issues we are going through in our daily lives, such as financial struggles, divorce, or bereavement.

And we can't understand why they don't understand what it is we want them to do or how we want them to behave.

Just as their childlike innocence and inexperience make them clueless to how we are feeling and why, equally, we have become clueless to their emotions and the reasons behind their behaviours. Cue miscommunication and misunderstandings on both sides, resulting in tears and tantrums all round.

IT'S NOT OUR FAULT

In today's fast paced society, we are reacting to people, things, places, and events unconsciously in Auto Pilot Mode. Unfortunately, this includes our children.

This is where our parenting problems lie.

But how can we possibly stay calm, cool, and relaxed when our children are misbehaving?

The key lies in our CONFIDENCE!

When we are in control of our own emotions and not being led by them, or affected by the emotions of others, including our children, and when we have a plan of action to follow, such as a routine that we know will help us to do the right things, at the right time, for the right reasons, then we emanate unshakable, parenting confidence.

It's that deep conviction of knowing that we are doing our best that gives us the strength and energy to carry on, despite problems, tears, and tantrums.

We will always be faced with parenting challenges, but feeling confident in the midst of them is what will help us to raise happy, healthy, and successful children.

These problems are not our fault—all parents face them, no matter what they do or don't do.

We should never feel guilty or to blame when things inevitably go wrong or for pursuing our own interests and having a life of our own. Going to work to progress in our careers or to make money for our families to live is part of Proactive Parenting. Those are essential aspects of a healthy, balanced life that helps us to increase our own self-esteem and confidence. This is vital because, if we ignore our own fundamental needs in life, we do ourselves and our children a great injustice.

WHAT OR WHO IS TO BLAME?

When we lack self-confidence, we doubt ourselves and what we do constantly. We end up comparing ourselves to other parents and our children to other children. And in our quest to get it 'right', we make mistakes.

We end up confusing ourselves, fretting that:

Not enough discipline will lead to our children going off the rails. Too much discipline will damage their self-esteem.

Not enough freedom will stifle their growth and development. Too much, and something might happen that's out of our control.

Lack of stimulation we fear will turn them into couch potatoes. Too many extracurricular activities, and we feel like pushy parents.

Too much choice, and we are in danger of making them spoilt and ungrateful. Not enough material possessions, and we think that we are depriving them of what all their friends are getting!

There's a fine line between pushing our children to succeed and pushing them over the edge, and for us parents, it's a worrying, guilty time.

The problem with all of this uncertainty is that it not only affects our own self-confidence when it comes to parenting, but it affects our children's self-confidence too.

This is when we end up trying too hard and become Competitive Parents, or we give up trying and end up reacting to our children instead. This haphazard approach arises out of desperation amidst the chaos of dirty nappies, sleepless nights, school runs, homework, and extracurricular activities, and is intensified by all those other unfamiliar challenges we encounter daily as new parents.

This is exacerbated further by the deception that we're surrounded on the schoolyard or at soft play, by seemingly 'Perfect Parents' with 'Perfect Children'.

We all know those calm parents who effortlessly glide successfully through all the usual parenting challenges in a confident manner, leaving the rest of us to look on in awe and envy, wondering why we and our children are so different? This is the reason we lack confidence.

We keep comparing our children to other people's children and comparing ourselves to other parents.

This creates pointless competition, because every parent and child are unique.

What works well for our sister Jenny's child, won't necessarily work the same for our own, and what the other mums at the school do to manage their children's behaviour may not suit us or our children.

REGAINING CONFIDENCE

Parenting confidence is a knowing, not a showing.

There's no need to compete with others or try to prove how good a parent we are to anyone.

The only person we need to prove our confidence to is our children.

Routines and rules can give us the confidence to manage our children's behaviour.

If, however, we doubt our ability as parents or we feel influenced by others to respond to our children's behaviour in a certain way, then our children will pick up on this fear or doubt.

This could be detrimental to our confidence and parenting abilities. Our children may use it to their advantage to get their own way. They may also come to lack confidence and trust in us, resulting in them misbehaving more.

It's easy to overreact to unwanted behaviour, but this doesn't make us look, act, or feel confident to either ourselves or in front of others or our children. It's usually those 'others' who are causing us to overreact to our children's behaviour in the first place. We then further complicate an issue by overreacting through embarrassment.

Our children will often embarrass us, so the best way to keep our composure is to expect it as normal.

Children often hit other children, say embarrassing things, and grass their parents up when they tell a fib. They actively love looking for ways to humiliate us in public—that is what they do, whether intentionally or unintentionally.

If we learn to walk our talk, that shouldn't bother us too much as there shouldn't be too many fibs or ways in which they will be able to humiliate us.

However, if they do find a way, it's not what they do or say that should concern us, but how we react to it and deal with them as a result. So, let's keep confidently cool.

More often than not, we will be more concerned with how others view us as parents and how they see us managing our children's behaviour than our children's behaviour itself.

Therefore, it's best to choose our battles wisely, but this takes a lot of confidence in our own parenting ability.

Knowing when to overlook certain, unwanted behaviour in our children and knowing when to step in at other times is an art.

(Don't worry, you can learn how to hone that over time by reading my other book, *The Powerful, Proactive, Parent's Guide to Present Parenting* if that's an area you would like help in.)

That's why it's always best to know our own boundaries and to set rules and routines that our children are familiar with regarding behaviour. They need to know what we expect of them. When we all know the rules, everyone will know how to act or react.

Let's take a typical scenario as an example, let's say you and your child are walking home from school together with your friend and their child. Your friend's child and your child are jumping in puddles that they find along the way. They are laughing and splashing about full of the joys of childhood when your friend charges over to them, demanding that they stop, as they are getting wet and splashing water everywhere.

Your child, however, carries on splashing regardless. Now, however, your child no longer seems to you like they are playing and having fun, now they seem to be influencing your friend's child to carry on jumping in the puddles against his mother's wish. At that point, you feel compelled to step in and tell your child off too and to stop them jumping in the puddles for fear of your friend judging you or your child's behaviour. You do this even though, deep down, you believe that your child is not misbehaving, just letting off a little steam after school and having some fun with their friend.

This lack of confidence in your own parenting abilities or beliefs about behaviour then causes your child to become confused as to why you are telling them off and trying so desperately to stop them having a good time?

If you normally allow them to jump in puddles, they will be thinking: 'What have I done wrong?'

You cannot, of course, explain to them in front of your friend that your friend doesn't like their behaviour or accuse them of misbehaving if you or your child do not believe that they are misbehaving.

On the other hand, say you stick to your integrity of firm, fair, consistent rules and allow your child to carry on playing in the puddles, you will then worry that your friend will think that you let your child get away with misbehaving or feel anxious that your child is negatively influencing her child to misbehave.

Although it's actually the opposite and is more to do with your friend influencing you with her rules which are different in comparison with your own.

Of course, if they are rudely splashing passers-by on purpose, that's a different matter, then, naturally, this issue needs addressing, but if they are wearing wellies and simply splashing a bit of water, what's the issue?

When we become confident in our own beliefs around behaviour and have our own set of rules, our own common sense will be able to guide us.

There's no one right way to manage behaviour, every parent and child is unique. There's no need for following, copying, criticizing, or listening to other people's well-meaning opinions. We have to trust ourselves and believe we are doing the best that we possibly can for our children, and then we will find the right solutions.

Children misbehave for all sorts of reasons, often they are just over excited, confused, scared, or unsure how to behave. They need to have confidence in us as their parents that we will correct them for the right reasons. By demonstrating self-confidence as a parent, our children will feel more safe and secure, and along with rules and routines, they will learn how to behave appropriately.

Routine is what this book will deal with specifically and being proactive as parents.

This means providing for our children's needs in advance, as opposed to dealing with issues when it's too late and our children desperately need something.

Although it's never too late to implement routines into our children's daily lives, its often far easier to proactively pre-empt misbehaviour when a routine is established early on.

CONFIDENCE IS THE KEY

If, however, we have an older child who doesn't already have a strong routine with rules in place, we need not feel victimized, guilty, ashamed, or embarrassed, confidence is the key to setting us free.

Confidence, however, is not something we are born with; it's something we acquire over time.

We certainly cannot train or practice parenting confidence before having children, it's an 'on the job' learning process.

The good news is, the more challenges we face and overcome the more our confidence grows stronger every day.

That is, once we realise we don't have to be perfect parents or have perfect children and that our parenting challenges don't all need to have successful outcomes.

We learn a lot more from our mistakes than we do from doing something well. So, we can immediately start to relax and ease up on ourselves from now on. Just like our children, we are learning, and we are learning together.

We actually learn more on how to parent from our children than we do from anyone or anything else. And if we allow them to guide us, they will be our best teachers.

But self-confidence comes from within; we are not going to find it anywhere else, no friend, no book, no one, nowhere—just within ourselves.

That's why it's vital to believe and trust in our own abilities.

We can help ourselves do this by creating a map to follow so that navigating through unknown territory and rough storms becomes easier. We do this by following a routine such as the U URSELF routine outlined here in this book and being mindful on the journey along the way. Being Present when with our children and having consistent rules and routines gives us, as well as our children, a sense of love, security, and most importantly, direction. When we know where we are going, what we are aiming for, and why, we tend to get there in the end.

When it comes to our goal of raising happy, healthy, and successful children, routines will help to build our self-confidence and ensure success. They help us to know that we are doing the right things for our children at the right time and in the right way.

All of this boosts our parenting confidence, and instead of feeling helpless and confused, we feel in control of the situation and understand what we need to do to make things better or prevent problems arising in the first place.

SELF AWARENESS

When we can accept our children and ourselves and decide to be authentically who we really are, then we are able to relax and feel a sense of inner peace and true confidence.

For this, we need to be able to reflect on our own behaviours as parents, a lot of which have been adopted from our own parents and carers in the past.

These past influences can affect our confidence today.

If our parents were overly anxious or angry at us all the time, although often unconsciously, that's the way we will likely learn how to respond to our children. And this will determine how we respond to unwanted behaviour.

If we had a smacked bum when young, then it's natural in the heat of the moment to discipline our children in the same way. It's a learnt behaviour, if this was a method often used, it would have become normalised, meaning we don't see the harm in it, or even think to question it.

But if our children carry on misbehaving, despite receiving a smacked bum as a punishment, or we feel guilty for hurting our children with physical punishment, then we will know deep down this isn't an effective method of managing or modifying their behaviour. And this will have a negative effect on our parenting confidence.

The only solution we have is reflecting on ourselves and our own motives, and analysing the effectiveness of what we do with our children, down to our own unique family values, individual feelings, and doing what we intuitively feel is best. Not in comparison with our own parent's views or with the views of our partners, friends, and family, which is where we normally seek advice.

Other people's views tend to be biased or outdated, and with so many different conflicting opinions, we only end up becoming even more bewildered in the process. Old school values, such as 'Children should be seen and not heard' collide with modern beliefs, such as 'Let your child lead the way.'

This results in many of us desperately mixing all the information and advice from well-meaning others together. Then, in a panic, we try out everything and anything from 'naughty steps' to never saying 'no' to our children in an attempt to get it right. Sadly, this only serves to have the opposite effect—unwanted behaviour and unhappy or unhealthy children.

The secret to parenting confidence, as we now know, lies in trusting in ourselves as parents and knowing what to do for our unique children and when.

When we know what to do, chances are our children will too. We are the only ones who really know our own children, and as we know them best, we know what is best for them, no one else.

As they love and trust us more than anyone else, that puts us in a good position to discipline, love, teach, protect, guide, and care for them. Any other outside influences need not apply, we are their leader. As Confident, Proactive, Present, Parent's, it's not so much what we do that counts, what matters most is why, how, and when we do it.

It's the small consistent things we do that make all the difference to our children's health, happiness, and success in life, long term. It's not about grand gestures, expensive gifts, parties, holidays, or what extracurricular activities we offer them.

These positive experiences do make a difference to their wellbeing, but ultimately, being a loving parent, who offers time and a stable consistent routine, is the best gift that we can give our children.

These are the gifts that keep on giving, because while our children are young, the sense of love, security, belonging, value and comfort that they provide, will stay with them as adults, helping them to feel more confident in themselves, both now and in the future.

They gain their confidence from us and knowing that we are always doing our best for them.

This is where the U URSELF Routine proactively puts us in control, without being a controlling parent.

It gives a set structure to the day that is both beneficial to our children's health and well-being, and to our confidence.

No matter how unique, all children need exactly the same things to be happy, healthy, and successful; that is, parents and carers who love them unconditionally, who spend time with them, and a routine that helps to build their esteem and includes Recreation and Exercise, Sleep, Love, and Food. That's what the U URSELF Routine is all about.

If we can provide all of that, we can be confident knowing that we are always doing our best, and that is always good enough.

KEEPING UP IS KEY TO CONFIDENCE

Parenting confidence is an on-going process that doesn't stop once we get into the swing of it. We have to be proactive by constantly keeping up with our children.

The relationship we have with our children consists of constant change. There will always be a new stage or phase around the corner, always a new parenting challenge we have not yet come across, and always new recommendations or fads thrown at us. All providing us with different issues and experiences.

If we have more than one child, then this keeping up is a lot more demanding, as no two siblings are ever the same. Each child is unique, and they individually change how we live our lives in different ways, and likewise, they are each affected differently by life.

This can all affect our level of parenting confidence at times. Being able to recognize, accept, embrace, adapt, and respond positively to those changes each child brings is the only option we really have.

It can be a challenge to keep up with their constantly changing preferences and behaviours, but that's the key to confident parenting.

And thank goodness for change. After all, who wants to be stuck in the terrible twos stage forever?

The good news is, amongst the chaos of all this change and uncertainty, every other parent on the planet is in exactly the same position as you.

The only difference between those parents who look like they've got parenting all sussed and those who don't is the level of proactivity they practise in their children's lives; in essence, how they provide routines.

CHAPTER 2:
THE U URSELF ROUTINE

WHAT IS THE U URSELF ROUTINE?

THE U URSELF ROUTINE is designed to help children feel good. Feeling good about themselves is crucial to being happy, heathy, and successful and is the core goal of this book and it's outlined routine. That's why Esteem is part of the U URSELF Routine.

The U URSELF routine also allows us to take charge and to feel Confident and Proactive as parents, guiding us in what we should be doing and when, just as much as our children. That's why it's such an effective and valuable parenting tool. When followed consistently on a daily basis, the U URSELF Routine helps us deduce a lot from our children's behaviour. For example, if they have had enough sleep, we can rule out them being tired when they misbehave or get upset, but if we know that they have not had enough sleep, then we will be able to see where the problem lies.

Routines also help us to proactively pre-empt our children's behaviour beforehand so we can plan and accommodate for those times when there have been interferences in their routines. For example, if we know they have not had their nap, we can avoid taking them to soft play until after they have had a nap.

Having this knowledge helps us limit a lot of unnecessary upset, not only for our children, but for ourselves too. Over time, with a consistent approach to the U URSELF routine, becoming over tired, starving hungry, bored, or attention seeking will be almost eliminated most of the time as the routine meets those needs in advance before it's too late.

By offering our children food before they are hungry or by putting them down for a nap just before they desperately need one, we help them to feel understood, cared for, and content. This prevents tears and tantrums for both parent and child because trying to soothe an over tired baby to sleep is a very stressful time for all in earshot, so it's never a good idea to wait until it's too late.

Carve the path for your child to walk or tread the hot coal's that follow, it's up to you.

Only you know what is best for you and your child and your family as a whole. Each and every family has their own way of doing things and their own setup. Therefore, it's you yourself who will ideally decide the routines you want your child to follow.

I have used with great success the U URSELF Routine with my own children and countless other parents that I have worked with.

It's one routine as a whole that comprises of seven different, yet co-dependant aspects. In order for you to remember the seven aspects of the routine, below is a useful mnemonic to help you, using the words 'You Yourself' abbreviated, and spelt U URSELF. These combined are what I refer to as the U URSELF routine.

1   **U = U time**
2   **U = Us time**
3   **R = Recreation**
4   **S = Sleep**
5   **E = Esteem**
6   **L = Love**
7   **F = Food**

Those seven, separate, yet co-dependent, routines combine into one solid tried and tested routine. They offer an outline of what every child needs, and why, to be happy, healthy, and successful.

Individual in their own right, each topic is co-dependent on one another, because it's pointless addressing our children's behavioural issues if we aren't addressing their sleep issues. Each aspect of our children's lives impacts one another, there's no point addressing your child's sleeping habits if you don't look at their exercise and recreational habits too. And like a missing piece of the puzzle, leaving out one area will fail to give us the whole picture. All the pieces or parts of the routine need to be collectively addressed at the same time.

We all do it, we focus on an area we feel is the problem and either buy a book dedicated to treating that problem area or tackle that area head-on with or without the help of others, but fail to find the solution we are after.

We need to encompass our children's habits as a whole in all areas, even those areas we are happy with that cause our child no issues.

They may be a good eater but what are they eating and when?

This can all have an impact on their quality of sleep and be an underlying cause of their sleep problems.

However, The U URSELF Routine will not tell you specifically what to do and when in each area. The specifics are always up to you to decide what best suits you and your individual child. The U URSELF routine will, however, be a useful, informative, motivational guide, providing ways in which you can effectively use the routine, and the reasons why each aspect of the routine is important.

Even though much of it is common sense, having a motive, or understanding the benefits of each aspect will give you the motivation and knowledge to stick to the routine, particularly when times become challenging.

If consistently followed, The U URSELF Routine is a reliable blueprint to guide you, but not if it's just on paper. You can read about it, and I can keep writing about it until we are blue in the face, but without taking action to implement it, it's worthless common knowledge. You have to be proactive in encouraging and following it with your child. So, let's begin.

WHEN AND HOW TO START A ROUTINE

I'm sure you're eager to begin implementing routine in your child's life by now.

Before we charge straight in, there's some pointers to consider first.

Twelve points to be precise, which are as follows.

1. Start Now
2. Be Patient
3. Be Understanding
4. No Punishment or Reward
5. Big up the Benefits
6. Warnings and Reminders
7. Stick to your Guns
8. Difficulties and Disruptions
9. Keeping it Real
10. Routine Review
11. Stay Strong and Persevere
12. Be Prepared

1.   START NOW

It's never too soon to introduce routine in our children's lives, the younger they are the better. Starting healthy eating, sleeping, and activity routines from birth is best but not essential.

Starting now and starting as we mean to go on is the proactive parent's motto for success!

Establishing routines early on integrates them as a normal and natural part of our children's lives. Even if you haven't given birth yet, preparations and decisions concerning routines can start now, the earlier the better.

Babies adapt quickly and are more accepting of routines than older children because:

- They know no other way and haven't had the chance to form bad habits.
- Routines help them to make sense of their chaotic new world.
- They are unable to independently meet their constant needs.
- They are unable to verbally communicate their needs to us.

We can find it difficult to know what they want, when, and why. Especially if we are new to the world of parenting, but with a routine, we can work it out.

Don't wait and put off a routine until you feel like they are old enough to understand. A six- week old baby is more inclined to sleep alone in their own bed and accept and understand a bedtime routine, than a six- year old that's used to co-sleeping and going to sleep at whatever time we retire to bed.

Having said that, if you have a six -year old and not a baby, it's still better to set a routine now, whatever their age, rather than not at all. The specifics of routines will always change over time anyway, but it's easier to change their routines than it is to suddenly create them from nowhere.

Our children can easily adapt to going to bed an hour later as they get older. But try telling a seven-year-old to go to bed an hour earlier than they are used to because of a new routine we want to start and we'll find this will be just as much of a challenge for us as it will be for our children.

2.   BE PATIENT

In the beginning, implementing any new routine will require patience, energy, and understanding on everyone's part.

The secret to successful routines will largely depend on how patient we are at carrying them out and how we encourage our children to follow them.

It means showing unconditional love, even when they refuse to eat the dinner that we've lovingly cooked for them and giving them enough time to practice getting used to their new bedtime routine by preparing them for bed a little earlier in the evening.

Trying to introduce more than one new routine a time is going to be difficult for any child to understand, like, or accept to begin with.

Start by introducing one new routine at a time, and start as you mean to go on (remember our motto?).

We may feel frustrated with our children when they won't go to bed when we tell them to, however, we still have to be patient in how we handle the situation.

It's tempting to expect them to change overnight because we want them to, but children won't change if we force or rush them.

Routines present opportunities to learn new and better ways of doing things, but they are best carried out in a calm, relaxed, and patient manner. Telling them off or rushing them to eat their meal is unproductive. The priority is on our children eating a well-balanced, overall diet and enjoying the mealtime experience. Not making them sit at the table trying to force them to eat their vegetables or clear their plate.

Each child and circumstance are different, but most, if not all, children will get used to routines when they can digest them in their own time.

Big disclaimer here though, no routine should become more important than our children's health or happiness. The whole point of routine is to help our children, not to punish them in any way. Sometimes it may take a while for them to understand that routines are for their own good. We just have to learn how to be patient and understanding to how they are feeling until they do.

3. BE UNDERSTANDING

Trying to understand that new routines can seem unfair to our children, and realising that they have only developed their current habits because we have let them, can be difficult.

By allowing our children to --- (please feel free to fill in the blank and insert whatever it is that you have allowed your child to do, for example, eat chicken nuggets every day or bed share for the last six years with you), then acknowledging that, intentionally or unintentionally, you have allowed it to become part of their normal routine, and now they know no other way, is a vital first step in changing things. It's a habit we've either allowed, created, or continued—or how else did it last so long?

Knowing this, we have to expect some resistance to change. Understanding before we begin that introducing a new routine is not going to be an easy transition for anyone. Particularly not for our children. We might know what we are trying to achieve and see the bigger picture, but they won't.

We know we are not changing their routine to hurt or punish them. Still, we need to be mindful of their feelings and empathetic in our approach, without feeling sorry for them. We can still let them know that we understand how they are feeling about the sudden changes and can empathize, but we don't want to sympathize. What we are asking them to do is not something horrible, we are introducing routines for their own good, out of love.

Whatever changes we endeavour to make, our message should be clear to our children, it's not a bad change in circumstances, it's just different!

4. ROUTINE PUNISHMENT

If we scold them whenever our children fail to comply, then we run the risk of making routines look more like punishments. We shouldn't display our anger when they don't follow their routines. We wouldn't be angry over them refusing cake that we offer out of love, and it's the same with their routines. They are a token of our love, and our children will come to love them also if we never use them as punishment.

It's common to hear parents threaten their children with:

'If you don't behave, you'll go to bed early' or 'If you don't eat your dinner there will be no dessert.'

Since when has going to bed or eating dinner been a punishment?

For us parents, eating and sleeping are usually the best parts of our day.

We want our children to look forward to returning to bed after a long day just as we do, and to enjoy their dinner as much as dessert.

If we threaten them with bed as a punishment or bargain with them to eat their dinner before dessert, then they'll come to think that going to bed is a punishment and dessert is a reward for enduring nasty vegetables!

5.   BIG UP THE BENEFITS OF ROUTINE

Instead, it's best to explain the benefits of routine to our children in an age appropriate way that they'll understand so they know that we are trying to help them, not punish them in any way.

This way, they are more likely to cooperate and adjust to their routines. If we can point out and prove the benefits of a routine, and explain how it's a natural, necessary part of every child's day in ways they understand, then life will be a lot easier.

Some children will be motivated by rewards and benefits, if your child is one of those children, then highlight the benefits of following their routine. Others are motivated by not losing out or by not being negatively affected by their actions. If your child is one of those types, explain to them the negative consequences of not following a routine. This will help them to avoid those negative consequences.

We are not trying to make our children feel guilty or scared in any way, just helping them to associate their behaviour and actions (or inactions as the case may be) with the consequences. But keep it positive and big it up at all times, the benefits to any routine should always outweigh the consequences of not following the routine.

This is something they may be unable to do alone. For instance, each time they stay up late at night and struggle to get out of bed for school the next morning, we can point out that they are tired because they went to bed late, and if they go to bed on time in the future, then they will wake up a lot easier, feeling a lot better.

Or if they've refused to eat dinner and a couple of hours later become hungry, irritable, or emotional, we can point out that their feelings are a result of hunger, and next time they will be a lot happier if they eat their dinner.

It's a good idea to keep a balance between the positive reasons for following the routine and the negative reasons for not. This means, if they refuse to go to bed, we can point out the positive reasons why they should and highlight the negatives of staying awake, so a typical example could sound like this:

'Go to sleep now, Sam, or else you will be too tired to play with your friends at nursery tomorrow and that won't be any fun. You need plenty of sleep to give you energy so you can climb that big climbing frame when you go to the park with Granddad in the afternoon too. So, the sooner you go to sleep, the quicker tomorrow will come and you can show him how high you can climb. But you won't be able to if you are too tired.

It may seem like a long -winded way to say 'Go to sleep,' but it's the quickest and most effective way in the long run.

Highlighting the positives and negatives encourages our children to want to follow routines a lot more than just telling them to comply or else. Providing an explanation helps them to know exactly why it benefits them and why we want them to go to sleep.

When they understand the benefits to them, routines then make sense.

6.   WARNING & REMINDERS

Even when children are familiar with and understand the benefits of their routines, if absorbed in play or watching their favourite TV programme, they won't welcome the interruption those routines bring. Those things they enjoy doing will always outweigh the benefits of going to bed. Unfortunately, that's life! They have to get used to it, but we can make it easier for them to accept. The best way to do that is to give them plenty of warnings and reminders. The worst way is to suddenly end their fun.

For example, if their bedtime is at seven and as soon as the clock turns, we abruptly say to them, 'Come on, time for bed now!'

This can be an unwelcome surprise.

We need to gradually prepare our children with warnings and reminders first. Letting them know fifteen to ten minutes beforehand that it's nearly time for bed gives them the chance to mentally and physically prepare themselves.

Young children have no concept of time, it's pointless saying they have ten minutes then forgetting to warn them until the time is up. Instead, we need to keep on reminding them at intervals, starting with:

1. Ten minutes—'Pack away your toys now, it is almost time for bed.'
2. Five minutes—'Go and brush your teeth before bed.'
3. Two minutes—'Let's have a kiss, ready for bed.'
4. One minute—'Jump into bed for your bedtime story.'

Or at mealtimes:

1. Ten minutes—'Let's turn the TV off, food's almost ready to eat.'
2. Five minutes—'Wash your hands before eating.'
3. Two minutes—'Sit at the table, food's coming.'

Preparation is vital in helping children wind down and feel ready for when the time finally arrives. Communication doesn't have to be verbal though, for babies, words won't be able to prepare them, but having before bed routines, such as bath, massage, cuddle, and bottle, will.

7.   STICK TO YOUR GUNS

Our children may not always welcome their routines with open arms, but we know how important they are to our children's overall wellbeing. That knowledge gives us the confidence to stand firm and stick to our guns when conflict arises.

I've met lots of children who lack routine in their daily lives, but I've yet to meet one child who hasn't benefited from some sort of daily routine. I assure you, if you hang in there and stick to your guns, everyone will benefit.

This means, often, you'll be hanging on a thread as your patience frays, but if seven o clock is bedtime, then our children should go to bed at seven every evening. Routine is all about doing the same things at the same times. However, there's no need to get neurotic if their bedtime is seven pm and they are still brushing their teeth at seven fifteen.

It's normal for children to stall going to bed.

They all mysteriously get this sudden urge to discuss events that happened in their day. Conveniently, these important matters can never wait, even though they've forgotten to mention them for the last six hours or more!

To resolve such stalling, all we need to do is to let them know calmly that in future, they will need to get ready for bed a little earlier, allowing them more time to chat about their day or brush their teeth.

They may be a little more reluctant to chat about insignificant things when they realise it'll take up the last few minutes of their playtime or take away time for their bedtime story in the evening.

Alternatively, you may find that your child is not dawdling deliberately to stay up later, but taking their time because they are tired and may actually need to go to bed a bit earlier in future.

In any case, if we expect our children to stick to their routines, we have to stick to them too. If we fall short in one area, say, finishing work late, delaying our children's meal, then the chances are, not only our children's mealtime routine will be late, but their bedtime routine also. Like a domino effect, a change in one can have a knock-on effect to every other routine.

8.   DIFFICULTIES & DISRUPTIONS

There will always be occasions when things don't go to plan. When it's inevitable that routines will be disrupted or difficult to stick to. Even well-established routines become disturbed at times, for all sorts of reasons.

Sometimes, it's sensible to allow them to be relaxed, but only with good reason, as this can result in our children acting out of character.

Sickness, late nights, holidays, celebrations, bereavement, starting school/ day care, visitors, and general problems at home can all have an impact on our children's routines, causing havoc in the process. Some interruptions to routine such as accidents or unexpected visitors are unavoidable and can't be anticipated or planned for. But, if we do know in advance that a visitor to the home is going to interfere with our child's routine or a future event is about to unfold, then we can proactively warn them in advance while making adjustments to minimise disruption. Disruptions are inevitable from time to time, although inconvenient, we can know this and can understand what's going on. We can also feel okay about the situation, but our children may not. Routines directly affect them, so they can feel confused, tired, hungry, or overwhelmed and, worst of all, powerless over what happens to them.

These disruptions should always be taken into consideration, especially if our children's behaviour has become disruptive as a result. Understanding the cause of our children's behaviour can help us to deal with the behaviour more appropriately and effectively.

Whatever the disruptions to routine may be, the most important thing we can do is settle them back into their usual routine as soon as possible or create a new one if needs be.

This can be difficult if the disruptions affect us too.

We may not always have the strength to persevere if we are not feeling good. For example, if bereavement has caused a routine to become unsettled or neglected, then chances are, we will also be affected by this in some way.

SINGLE PARENTS

I have found it not uncommon for parents who have recently split up to turn to their children for comfort. Often allowing them to stay up later or bed share with them. This is usually justified by thinking that their children are feeling insecure and need them. This is right, they probably do, but in most cases, the truth is, the newly single parent needs the child to need them as they are feeling rejected or sad. There's nothing wrong with needing some love when we are feeling low, as long as we know that's what's happening and why.

And understand that it's not our children's fault when we find happiness again and decide we no longer want them to stay up late or bed share with us and try to change that.

Now, I'm not picking on single parents here. I admire them most (I myself grew up in a one parent family without my Mum) as they have to do all this parenting routine stuff alone, often with little or no support. But I can't help noticing that when some parents split up, a competitive game can ensue between the two.

They say children always suffer when parents use them in their games (really, this is a game no one wins) but I've found children are the only ones who really ever win at this game as they learn how to play one parent against the other. Parents wanting to be the 'best parent' often give in to their children. That normally means allowing them to stay up late, eat treats, and have gifts for no reason. Routine especially falls by the wayside when the absent parent who only has limited time such as weekends to spend with their child wants to 'make the most of their time together'.

The poor parent who spends most of their time with the child, tirelessly providing a routine, then has to suffer the rest of the time with a tired child. A child who often prefers their other parent as they do more fun things and give them what they want. If you are at the receiving end of this from an ex- partner and parent to one of your children, then as a proactive parent, you have to address it. This is a stressful situation as the other parent may use this against you. You may understandably worry they might deliberately go against your wishes and flout your routines as a way of getting you back for past hurts.

It's likely they may try; on the other hand, they may be totally unaware of the problems they are causing and may well apologise and try to help you. They may have only been doing it out of a genuine, misguided love for your child. And their motives may innocently stem from wanting to spend happy time with them or as a result of them trying to compensate out of guilt for not being around as much anymore.

In either instance, your child's health and happiness is what's most important. If in any doubt, proactively pass this book onto the other parent so you are both on the same page.

9. KEEPING IT REAL

Certain routines and their timings will be personal to each individual child within a family. One child may be younger, making their bed time different from their older siblings, and this is where difficulties can lie.

They may resist being the only one going to sleep early, and we can't force them to sleep. But we still have to insist on them following their bedtime routine. We have to tell them to go to their room to sleep and make sure that they are in bed at the right time.

As long as they stay in their bed, whether they sleep or not is ultimately up to them (but don't worry, using this same approach every night, and going to bed at the same time, eventually, will be all the cue they need to fall asleep naturally, in fact, they'll come to expect it!).

The younger the child, the easier and quicker this will be. It's the same with mealtimes. If they don't want to eat, then all we can do is offer them a healthy nutritious meal and let them decide to eat it or not? We can't actually do it for them or force them to do anything. We just need to provide the routines for our children to follow as best they can, then our part as loving, responsible, Proactive Parents is done.

10. REVIEW ROUTINES

Over time, our children's needs will change. If a routine has stopped working, then these changes will need to be reflected in their routines. A three-year-old will naturally need less sleep than when they were a baby, and a ten -year old may not be tired at six pm anymore.

By reviewing routines regularly, we can see what's still suitable and what's not. This way, knowing we are doing the right thing for the right reasons at the right time means we can feel confident and stick to the routines we have set, even when our children try to change them.

We have parental responsibility over our children for good reason. Change or abolish their routines they may try, but the onus is on us to stay strong and persevere.

11. STAY STRONG & PERSERVERE

We shouldn't give up and let our children's defiance toward their routines discourage us. By persevering and keeping routines going regardless, whether our children follow them or not, we provide the regularity and certainty that they need in their life. Unquestionably, with practice and patience, routines soon become habits for most children, even the reluctant ones.

Children can, however, be very creative in their approach to flouting new routines, and also very wearing and persistent. I remember my own two little ones complaining at bedtime about the children who were younger than them playing outside in the street, and questioning me why they had to go to bed while the sun was still shining? Using guilt as their preferred tool of negotiation, protesting, 'I don't want to go to bed, it's not fair, the sun is still out.'

But I was confident that keeping to their bedtime routine, was good for them. That's how I managed to remain calm and stay strong and persevere.

It was hard though, I must admit. But had I felt guilty and uncertain that what I was doing was unfair, I may have succumbed and given in, allowing them to stay up a little later.

That would have been a BIG mistake!

If we succumb to our children's guilt trips and move the goal posts just once, then we can expect them to move them even further the next time as they try to find out how far they can push things in their favour.

Guaranteed, next time, they will use that as their trump card. If we do succumb, we have to prepare ourselves to be subjected to most children's favourite phrase, you know, the one that makes most parents cringe in annoyance at themselves: 'It's not fair, you let me yesterday, why not today?'

To which, no parent can ever find a justifiable explanation.

So, we either end up giving into them once again, creating another unwanted habit that's hard to break or, we become annoyed and upset with ourselves, for giving in to them in the first place, resulting in a no win for us parents, but possible triumph for our little ones! Once we've allowed something once, there's usually no going back.

REVELLING IN THE RESULTS

That's why it's best to persevere and stay strong from the outset. If we can persevere with routines until we get the results we want, then life will become much easier for ourselves, as well as our children. Other parents and their children (such as those playing outside at bedtime) may take a different approach.

And that's fine for them. After all, they're the ones who will be responsible for their own children's health and well-being and managing their own children's behaviour. But you will be responsible for your children, no one else's. Focusing on the most beneficial, proactive approach that's suitable for you and your child is always best. This, I may add, is not the easiest approach initially. But I promise, long term, you'll be revelling in the results. Keeping consistent is key, routines are then fair and make sense. And when they make sense to our children, the sun may have his hat on, but our children will try to sleep anyway!

12. BE PREPARED

As the old adage goes, 'No plan is a plan to fail'. So, let's be prepared with a plan of action. The U URSELF routine is the best plan I've found to work with the children I've cared for, but feel free to find your own.

Whatever routine you use, there'll be times along the way (likely when you're scraping a meal you've spent hours, lovingly preparing into the bin! Or when, your unappreciative child is moaning about an activity or outing you've arranged for them as part of Us time together) when you will wonder why you are bothering.

This is perfectly normal; most routines are basic and straight forward, but that's not to say they will always be easy.

If you are prepared for those times and stick with it and are consistent in your approach, you will soon see why you bothered, and you will be glad that you did!

We just have to take it one day at a time. No matter how much we prepare our children or no matter how prepared we think we are, we will still find implementing routines difficult at times. That's why we need to choose a time to introduce any new routines when we are feeling both mentally and physically strong and determined. It's easier for us to give up and give into our children if we are tired or frustrated ourselves.

Parents constantly tell me that the reason why they gave up on a routine was because of their children's resistant, unwanted behaviour toward the routine. Whatever the particular issues that they were having, whether it was eating or sleeping problems, what they are saying is that they found their children's behaviour too much for them to handle. It's a scary thought that a child can have that much control over an adult, but it's very common.

Unfortunately, every time we give in to our children, we hand them over a little more power and create a habit that's hard for them to break. But more than that, giving in to them also means any effort made previously in trying to establish a routine was all in vain and a total waste of time, tears, effort, and energy.

Fortunately, the parents I know who have introduced their children to the U URSELF Routine and have followed the suggestions set out here in this book, tell me that their children love the new routine and are happier, healthier, and more successful as a result.

And why wouldn't they be, it's to benefit them, after all.

What child wouldn't want more time, understanding, love, and attention?

And what parent wouldn't want that for their child?

I'm not here to advise you on specifics such as what time your child should go to bed—that's for you to decide. What's important is understanding our children's habits and being able to influence or change them in order to steer them down the healthier, automatic highway, leaving you more time for you!

CHAPTER 3:
U TIME—U COME FIRST

U TIME IS EXACTLY that—time for 'You.'
It comes first in the U URSELF Routine because 'You' are the most important part of the routine and the most important person in your child's life.

WHO CARES FOR YOU IF YOU DON'T?

Life has a funny way of slowing us down and making us conscious at times.

Recently, I had a minor operation on my foot which forced me to literally keep my feet up for a few days. I was frustrated by the inconvenience to say the least!

That was until I realised the perfection in the problem.

I had been struggling to find time to focus on my accounts and finish editing my latest book for months, and I was almost worn out with everything I had to do, then, suddenly, I was forced to put my feet up and relax.

And guess what?

I finished those accounts in a weekend, made significant progress with my book, and I had a lot of shut eye to boot. I also had time to think. Time to appreciate all those things we usually take for granted. Hidden treasures, such as the sound and glow of a crackling fire on a cold day, the taste of tea and warm toast dripping in butter, the smell of clean, fresh laundry blowing on the washing line and the comfort of crisp cotton sheets on your bed at night.

Each day presents us with an array of beautiful moments that can easily go by unnoticed by our everyday senses. Our health is something we rarely consider when we are so busy, and it's certainly something we all take for granted until we become ill or are unable to function physically or mentally in some way. I constantly see and hear individuals apologising that they need a break from helping others and from social media, but it's not something any of us should feel guilty about. Self-care should be our priority first and foremost, I mean who cares for YOU if you don't?

Feeling our body's discomfort and not being able to do what we want is the surest sign from Life that it's time to slow down. It also gives us the space and time to think about our daily lives, including those habits we rarely, if ever, notice.

And these habits are not all bad!

On this day, as I'm writing this, I'm finally going to be free of my sutures (stiches) and able to enjoy a nice, warm, bubble bath. Ahhh... the bliss hidden in the simple everyday things in life that we all take for granted.

We all need time out now and again. Even the most gregarious amongst us need some alone time to plan, ponder, reflect, and recuperate. But we needn't wait until we are forced or it's too late!

Making 'U Time' should be an everyday priority. And that includes taking care of our physical health and appearance, sleeping well, eating clean, exercising, meditating, learning, laughing, and spending time with those we love, doing what we love most. Something life was telling me to get back into alignment with but I hadn't been listening to while I was chasing my goals.

WHO CARES FOR YOUR CHILD IF YOU CAN'T?

Anyone who has ever flown on an aeroplane will be familiar with the safety drill, where the Stewardess asks you to make sure you put on your own safety vest and masks before your children's or anyone else's. Taking care of 'You' is a priority because if you don't, then you won't be able to care for your child or anyone else. Yet many of us selfless parents still think it's okay to put the needs of others, especially our children's, before our own. We are not being selfish by taking care of our own needs before anyone else's, it's essential.

If we take care of our own needs and wellbeing and pursue our own interests, then not only our own happiness, health, and success will be positively affected but noticeably our children's too.

A happy parent equals a happy, contented child.

As parents, we should never neglect or underestimate the importance of time for ourselves, so do not skip this vital part of the routine. After all, if we can't stick to a simple routine of taking time out for ourselves each day to relax and recuperate, then how can we expect our children to do the same and follow their routines?

It's time to find that U time for ourselves without feeling guilty, by:

- Looking at where we currently spend our time.
- Determining how we would rather be spending our time.
- Finding ways in which we can go about getting some of our time back by learning to say 'no' to Time Takers.
- Taking time out.

It's probably safe to assume that you will already have your own list of things that you would like to do, if only you had the time.

No one other than you can decide on the best ways in which to indulge in a little U time. From an uninterrupted soak in the bath, to the more ambitious dream of producing a film for the big screen, we all have things we would like to do more of.

BEFORE YOU BEGIN

Often, the problem's not having enough time for you to spend on yourself, but how much time you choose to use on yourself with the time that you do have.

So, before we begin, grab your notebook, pen, and a cuppa, and let's start our U Time now by taking some time to reflect on how we are actually spending our time.

WHERE DOES YOUR TIME GO?

We have to ask where our time is going and what we're doing that is actually more important than spending time on ourselves?

Try this simple exercise: make a list of all the things or people you spend your time on each day. Next to them, put how many minutes or hours you dedicate to each one. Here's an example of my lists on a typical working day:

1. Sleeping 6 hours
2. Work 10 hours
3. Housework 1hour
4. Time with my children 1hour
5. Studying 1hour
6. Writing /Reading 1hour
7. Having a bath 1hour
8. Therapy/ Coaching Sessions with clients 1hour
9. Watching TV 1hour
10. Time with my husband 1hour

Lists may vary from day to day. For example, on a Sunday I don't work, so would have ten hours to visit family and friends or go to my allotment.

It's almost impossible to segment each activity or person into a time slot as our time usually interlinks with more than one person or activity. I have only put one hour for time with my children and husband, but in reality, I spend a lot more of my time with them. But as I'm also working, caring for other children at the same time, I have listed only 1 hour of dedicated US Time for my children and husband.

The 'Where does your time go?' listing process should highlight time given to a particular person or purpose.

This way, we can see where most of our time is spent, and with this information, change how we use our time, especially where the time for something or someone is lacking, which is usually time for you!

Then if we want to meet a friend for coffee, we can swap an hour watching TV to do so.

The list physically shows us how we do have enough hours, we just need to choose what we feel is important to do with them.

MAKE EVERYDAY SPECIAL

U time doesn't have to be segmented into a free hour here or there, we can make our whole life more enjoyable if we use our time doing things that we like and want to do.

If we're honest, doing anything other than that is a waste of our precious time.

It's pointless only ever enjoying time for yourself when you are on holiday for four weeks of the year, and then enduring forty-eight weeks of hard graft and stress the rest of the time.

Living for the weekend to arrive or our summer holidays in order to relax and be happy robs us of the opportunity to live and enjoy life to the fullest. It's living half a life. If we could only plan our lives like we do Christmas or our summer holidays, then all that attention to detail, time, energy, money, and motivation to make it good would create a fabulous life.

Enjoying life shouldn't be reserved for those fun times and special occasions such as holidays or celebrations. It's about enjoying and appreciating every day, including those ordinary boring days like today when nothing extraordinary or special is happening... just your life!

PARENT TRAP
Sometimes we can fall into the parenting trap of being so focused on our children that we lose the desire to pursue our own dreams and ambitions.

If this sounds like you, then now would be a good time to list as many things as you can in ten minutes that you would like to do if only you had more time.

This will give you the clarity you need to discover what it is that you really want to do.

This list is not to include things such as spring cleaning your children's bedrooms. This is the time to list those things that will make you happy when doing them, for no other reason than pure pleasure or relaxation.

Things like investing in a spa day, taking up windsurfing, or whatever else happens to be your cup of tea. Try to be as adventurous as you can, but it's not necessary. Even reading a book or going for a walk are great ways in which to spend time on you. All that matters is that it's something for 'You' that 'You' really want to do.

MY U TIME LIST

1.
2.
3.
4.
5.
6.
7.
8.
9.
10.

LESS IS MORE

Armed with your U time list, you may now feel like you need even more time to enable you to do those extra things.

But it's not about finding more time to get more things done, or to tackle things you've been putting off.

It's about finding time for you to do less.

It's about being able to sit and gaze out the window at the world while you have a coffee, daydreaming.

It's doing less of those unenjoyable things so you can spend more time on you, doing things you do enjoy.

The buzz word of our time is multitasking, but if we actually did less instead of more, we would find that we actually get more done as a result of focused concentration.

If you feel as though you always have things to do, places to go, and people to see, it can feel like you are being stretched beyond your limit.

This scattering of your time and attention anywhere and everywhere can result in you going nowhere and doing nothing fast.

Normally, we do what we urgently have to do, as opposed to what we really want to do, meaning our actions are often directed by the proverbial gun.

This can often feel like someone is literally holding a loaded gun to our head, making everything suddenly urgent or life-threatening, which can lead to stress and anxiety.

Yet, a lot of this urgency is magnified by our own imagination.

Constantly feeling worried or hurried though can actually lead to real problems manifesting in our lives, which can affect our emotional and physical health and wellbeing. When we realise that, in reality, we are the only ones holding the gun to our head, no one else, and that actually, the gun is not loaded, it's only imaginary, then we release the pressure.

NO TIME LEFT FOR ME?

This imagined pressure that we impose on ourselves gives us the illusion that we have no time left for us. The real issue, however, is that most of us feel guilty about spending time on ourselves when there are so many other 'more important' things we feel that we have to or should do.

As luck would have it, there's nothing more important than spending time tending to our own needs, because if we don't have our own health and happiness, then we will lack the energy to take care of the most important people in our lives—our children.

That's why it's important to prioritise U Time in our diaries daily. Time just for ourselves to have a bath, read a book or magazine, enjoy a glass of wine, go out for a meal, or to the cinema, go for a massage, manicure, facial or acupuncture, take up a new hobby or educational course, join the gym or try a new sport. Do anything and everything you fancy just for fun daily, once a week is not enough.

Once we start using the U URSELF Routine and our children receive adequate US Time, Recreation, Sleep, Exercise, Love, and Food routines, we soon come to realise that we do have enough time for ourselves, and there's nothing to feel guilty about.

But before we go any further, the first step to U Time is going to be letting go of all that guilt.

Being a parent can be a guilty business if we let it, torturing us more than it can criminals. It's usually the most loving parents amongst us who experience it the most. If only we could extend that love onto ourselves more often than guilt?

If only our children felt this guilty whenever they woke us up in the middle of the night for no reason, or whenever they humiliated us with a tantrum in a busy supermarket.

But they don't. They love making us feel guilty, as it gives them ammunition to fire at us whenever they want to get their own way.

And no wonder they love this method so much, as it works so well when it comes to them getting their own way. No parent ever wants to see their child upset, and our children can pick up on this fact and be very clever and creative in instilling us with a guilty complex. So too can our boss, spouse, and even our own parents.

It's a technique, and each will have their own style:
- An angry style, 'It's all your fault!'
- A feeling sorry for themselves, 'It's all my fault.'
- Or the subtle style, done in a nice, yet underhanded way.

My daughter has a nice style. Instead of risking a 'no' and asking me outright for whatever she wants, she nicely instils guilt before-hand.

Such as the time she said to me:

'Oh, Mum, can you...? Oh, never mind, it doesn't matter.'

'What?' I asked, intrigued, in the middle of doing something else.

'Well I was going to ask if you would paint my nails, but I know you are too busy at the moment and I don't want to take up your time when you could be doing something more important.'

Horrified by her words, I instantly dropped what I was doing and happily painted all of her little fingernails, as I explained that I was never too busy to do anything for her.

In fact, I told her I enjoyed doing it.

It was only later as I guiltily mulled it over with my husband, that I realized I had nothing to feel guilty about.

When he pointed out to me that my Daughter knew exactly what she was doing, and she knew that what she said would make me feel guilty enough to do what she wanted me to do. I had fallen for the guilt trip, even though I had nothing to feel guilty about, as I had done her nails for her. Yet I was still carrying those words 'Too busy' with me while indulging in my guilty complex hours later.

I'm sure that if you are anything like me or the majority of other loving parents out there, then you too can feel guilty about almost anything and everything.

Guilty about working, not working, spending money on yourself, having a childfree night out, putting your child in childcare, saying 'No' to your child when they want something, telling them off/being too strict or too soft, not being able to afford the Christmas presents they want, choosing the wrong school, Mum/Dad for them, living in the wrong area, not taking them out on day trips/holidays or spending enough quality time with them, not realizing they were ill/being bullied/underachieving at school, making them do homework, not being able to make their school sports day/Christmas concert, lying about Fluffy the Hamster's demise up the vacuum cleaner!

Boring I know, but that guilty list is endless as a parent.

Feel free to carry on with your own long list, if you feel in the mood for making yourself feel like an awful parent.

In fact, you may find this exercise cathartic, even funny, who knows, let's try it?

GUILTY RUBBISH

- Grab your pen and notebook again and a cuppa while you're indulging in some guilty 'U Time'.
- Now, list as many things that you either have or have not done for your child, or about your role as a parent, as you can manage in the space of five minutes that makes you feel guilty.
- Think of everything that pricks at your conscience, tugs at your heartstrings, or tickles you as much as a bash on your funny bone. Go on, indulge in your guiltiness until you feel really bad. Let all that guilt flow, get it all out of you, out of your head and onto paper.
- And then .... rip that list up into tiny pieces and let it all go. Throw it away with all the other useless rubbish in the bin. Make sure you put it in the rubbish bin and not the recycling though; you don't want it coming back in some other form one day. You want it out of your life for good, out where it belongs with the rest of the rubbish, in the refuse dump until it disintegrates.

So, what? Maybe you're not as creative as some of the other parents at making costumes, and maybe your daughter did look more like Casper the Ghost than the Angel Gabrielle in her Nativity play, you don't need to feel guilty about that anymore.

WHO'S TO BLAME?

But before we start to blame our children for making us feel guilty (and end up making ourselves feel even more guilty for blaming them), let's not forget who taught them all they know.

Our children will have been taught by the 'Master Guilt Trippers' of all time, their very own guilty role models—us parents. We are all guilty of using guilty tactics when we need our children to do something that they do not want to. Popular statements being:

- 'If you don't hurry up and get ready then we are going to be late, and I will get fired from my job and we will have no money to pay the bills!'
- 'If you don't behave, Father Christmas won't bring you any presents.'
- 'Eat your greens, there are poor kids in third world countries starving to death who would give anything to have what you have.'
- 'I gave up so much to have you and you won't do this one favour for me?'

But the problem with guilt is, it makes everyone feel bad.

We want our children to willingly help and cooperate with us, not to feel bad if they don't, and vice versa.

There's always a better way of getting our point across or our requests met where no one feels guilty. We just have to practice releasing guilt as an option.

GUILTY BUSTER

Guilt is a waste of time and an emotion that's draining. Instead, we are better off channelling our energy into doing something to resolve issues that cause us guilt.

We can start by trying this guilt busting exercise and writing our answers down:

- Think of the thing that makes you feel guilty. For example, not reading a story to your child before bedtime.
- Ask yourself how long and how often have you spent your time feeling guilty about not doing it?

- And how long are you going to continue feeling guilty and punishing yourself over it?
- Then ask yourself why you just don't do it in the first place?

You may find the reason for not doing something that's making you feel guilty is lack of time?

Therefore, it may be just as quick, and feel a lot better, to just do the very thing, that you have no time to do, rather than waste the time and energy feeling guilty about not doing it.

- If you are still feeling guilty about anything that was on your previous list (that you should have by now thrown in the bin!) go through each thing on your list now and try and turn it into your guilty pleasure. Ask yourself what good reasons can you find for doing/not doing it?

For example, you may feel guilty because you often work late and miss reading your child a bedtime story.

But your good reason for working late is to pay the bills and buy your child the experiences and things they need to grow and develop.

Maybe you feel guilty over a night out with friends or a child-free weekend away?

But you can reassure yourself that time away from your child is exactly what you need to relax and be you again. Giving you the chance to miss them and enjoy their company more when reunited afresh.

This exercise can help you to understand that to regain your sense of self, you need this guilty pleasure.

As a consequence of using your time to do things you want to do, you will feel happier, making you a calmer, more content and relaxed parent.

We all need time and space away from our children occasionally if only to feel refreshed and able to cope with their everyday demands.

The truth is, even if we could give them a hundred hours a day, it would never be enough. Our children's need for our time and attention is insatiable, and can never be constantly met, no matter how hard we try or how much time we dedicate to them.

It's not selfish to satisfy our own needs or do what we have to do to provide the best life for our family. It's the one thing that prevents us feeling resentment toward our children for taking up all our time and energy. Therefore, it's the most loving thing we can do for ourselves and our children.

NEVER ENOUGH TIME

If all we live for is our children, then eventually, one day when they leave home and start a life of their own, we will be left without anything else in our lives but a vast void of emptiness.

If you feel that to be a good parent you should sacrifice your life, including your needs and desires, then making time for you may be difficult at first.

No doubt you will probably find a million excuses for why there is never enough time to do the things you say you want to do.

You may discover that your child taking up all your time and energy has become the perfect excuse not to do those things that you believe you want to do.

The truth is, everybody has twenty-four hours in a day, seven days a week, fifty-two weeks of the year, no exceptions.

The only difference is how we choose to spend our time.

- If it were announced on the news today by the Government that there was going to be twenty-six hours in a day from now on, and you had an extra two hours each day, would you still be too busy to find time for yourself?
- If so, why would you still be busy with an additional fourteen hours a week?
- What do you think you would do more of, and what would you do less of with the extra time?

Your answers may give you clues as to why you are currently too busy to find time for yourself and how gaining extra time may or may not make any difference to your life.

SAYING 'NO' TO TIME TAKERS

Picture this, it's a sunny Monday morning, and you're sat gazing out your window as you sip a warm, velvety, smooth coffee. The children are at the childminders, the housework is all complete, and the only noise you can hear are the birds singing. You've nowhere to go, nothing to do, no one to see.

This has got to be bliss!

If heaven were on earth this would surely be it, right?

But why does it sound like a fictitious fairy tale reserved for the Princesses out there, not Mums like us?

Because our minds won't allow us to switch off and just relax.

When there's nothing to do or worry about, it worries us, and we think that something must be wrong.

The still quietness makes us feel uneasy. Surely, Life can't be stress free, especially not on a Monday morning anyway.

There's always something that needs doing or someone who needs us. Besides, life would be boring sipping coffee all day anyway, we reassure ourselves as we rush off to find something to do somewhere.

And on cue, those Time Takers are ready and waiting to oblige. They are easy to recognise, as Time Takers need you, but you don't need them.

They come in all sorts of disguises and are not always people. They can be jobs that need doing, places we have to go to, commitments we don't need want or enjoy. Feel free to make your own list of Time Takers, as this will be invaluable in taking that time back in the future. Here are some examples to kick start you off:

- Your boss asks you to do over time.
- Your partner wants you to entertain their friends.
- The dog needs a walk.

- The school needs a volunteer.
- Family is coming to visit.
- There's a course you must take.
- A Friend wants a gossip.
- Email & Social Media notifications keep going off.
- Your Sister needs a babysitter.
- Your Dad needs help with the gardening.
- Your Mum needs a lift to the hospital.
- The housework/decorating needs doing.

All of these can feel like they urgently need attending to instead of doing something for ourselves.

And all are worthy, loving acts, but we don't have to be the one who attends to them all, all the time. Doing too much can feel like we're being stretched beyond our limit, and this scattering of time and attention, anywhere and everywhere, can result in us going nowhere and doing nothing fast.

When we know how we want to spend our time and who with, this allows us to say 'No' to other 'less important' things.

This stops us over committing ourselves to others when we have too much to do already.

It's about learning to say 'No' without feeling guilty or upsetting other people, and like anything else, it gets a lot easier the more we practice saying it.

'No' is a crucial word when it comes to 'You Time'.

We need to practice saying 'No' more often to others, and stop saying 'No' to ourselves.

Yet it's the one little word that we find the most difficult to say to other people, even when we do not have enough time and are feeling overstretched.

We may also find that we cannot say 'No' to other less important people in our lives as much as to the ones that we love.

People who love us already accept and understand us, so we are more inclined to try and please others who are not so important in our lives to gain their acceptance.

These people who demand our time are called 'Time Takers'. We don't have to be rude to anyone, but we do have to prevent them from stealing our precious time.

Whenever Time Takers ask for your time, simply say:

'I would have liked to have helped you out, but I am already doing something at that time that is really important to me'.

The more often you say it, the less often they will take your time. It's not being selfish to the needs of others or becoming self-centred or unloving, it's about valuing our own time. If we show others what our time is worth to us, they will start to appreciate it too.

'Time Takers' are stealing your precious time away from you and your loved ones. We wouldn't let them steal our children's dinner money, yet just like thieves in the night, we allow them to get in the way of their bedtime story.

We are not the one being selfish for choosing to spend some of our time on ourselves. It's those people who are demanding of our time who are thinking of themselves. Now, the occasional babysitting or lift here or there is fine. No one's saying we can't help out our family and friends when they need us. The issue arises when we feel people are demanding or they constantly rely on us to help them out.

If we think something is an obligation, or we feel guilty if we don't do something, or we are using these Time Takers as excuses not to tend to our own needs, then there's a problem.

Loving parents are caring and want to help others, but if we don't assert ourselves and take back some of our time, we will suffer as much as our children.

We are all responsible for our own lives, and we should take the responsibility and allow others to do the same. We can, however, turn much of our list of 'Time Takers' into 'You Time' if that's what we want to do.

Walking the dog, for example, offers fresh air to clear the head, and it's good exercise, however, if we feel overwhelmed with responsibilities and do not enjoy doing that, we come to resent it, especially if it's not our dog.

MIND YOUR OWN BUSINESS

Working late when we would rather be reading our children a bedtime story or going to aerobics instead is putting our boss's needs over our own. And our boss will always keep taking!

It's nothing personal, its business.

Our time is personal though, and worth more to us than our wages ever will.

We can always make more money, but we can never make more time, once it's spent, it's gone forever. If we use our time at work that we are paid for productively, then no one should expect more of us.

It's time to mind our own business, over-committing to others leaves us little time for ourselves, and before we know it, other people's problems can become our own.

When we start to get on with our own business and get less involved in other peoples' dramas, the days and weeks will start to flow, and everything will end up getting done, effortlessly, and in perfect time, as we concentrate on who and what matters most.

Lack of time will cease to be a problem, and we'll find more time to relax and enjoy life.

Others may not like this change in you, especially if you are in the habit of doing everything for everyone and always saying 'Yes'.

Most people will not like this newfound ability that you have acquired to say 'No'.

They may even try to make you feel guilty at first, but remember why they are called 'Time Takers', and you'll no longer feel guilty over them stealing your time.

Gradually, 'Time Takers' will diminish, and we will find ourselves offering others our assistance and time happily and willingly without being asked instead of grudgingly feeling like we have to.

We'll also be far more appreciated by others as well when we do offer our time.

TIME OUT

You may be surprised to find you don't know what to do with all that time at first?

Fear not, our children will be at hand to show us if we let them.

So, we need to clearly communicate the importance of time just for ourselves to them in a way that stops them from feeling rejected.

We can do this by explaining that we won't be able to devote time just for them later to do whatever activity they want to do with us if we don't finish what we need to do first.

We have to let them know in no uncertain terms that we expect them to leave us alone to get on with it. This is easier said than done.

Multi-tasking our children with other things is more time efficient but ignoring them and getting upset with them while doing other tasks is unproductive.

They don't end up getting the best from us, neither does the task we are trying to do.

We never need to feel guilty, as children also need U Time for themselves too.

Time with their own thoughts to play, ponder, and daydream is vital.

If they can learn to be comfortable alone with themselves, they will never be lonely or bored ever again.

It's a knack, although some children are naturally more reserved and introverted while others are inclined to need constant attention and stimulation.

But parenting is not about dedicating all of our time to our children and neglecting everything and everyone else in our life.

If we spend all day playing games with our children but haven't washed or ironed their uniform for school, then we haven't been very responsible or proactive in our approach to parenting.

Our children need more than a playmate from us, they rely on us for everything, including their clean clothes.

All children with time can grow to enjoy their own company, as long as they are given the opportunity to do so and receive adequate US Time, that is—time with us, which is what we'll spend some time on next.

We'll soon discover that after adequate Us Time, our children soon bore of us and demand our attention less, naturally stepping back a bit and giving us the space we need for U Time.

CHAPTER 4:
US TIME IS TIME WELL SPENT

US TIME IS VALUABLE

C HILDREN NEED AND WANT our attention, and they don't mind how they get it.

That means if they don't feel they're getting enough of it naturally, they will force us to pay attention to them, usually by misbehaving.

Just as we create rules and routines out of love for our children, they too misbehave to grab our attention because they love us.

The only way to remedy this is to make sure they receive adequate daily Us Time with us. This can be hard to measure, though.

QUANTITY VERSUS QUALITY TIME

A lot of emphasis over the past decade or so has been on spending 'quality time' with our children, but surely, we want to make sure we provide quality time for our children all of the time?

There's no point enjoying half an hour of happiness in the park, only to spend the rest of the day telling them off or being busy with other things.

Every minute together is precious time.

Time is priceless but can easily become worthless, depending on how we use it. As it's so valuable, it makes sense to spend it wisely, and time spent with our children is the best investment that we can make.

How much is your child worth to you?

- How much exactly is your child worth to you?
- How much would you want in exchange for your child, a hundred pounds, a thousand pounds, two million, maybe a billion?

I'm guessing no amount of money would be enough.

Our children are priceless, and the best way to show that we value them is by generously giving them our most valuable asset—our time.

If they understand that we value ourselves and our own time as well as valuing the time we spend with them, they will learn to value themselves.

The value that they place upon themselves is not dependent on possessions or monetary value. No number of treats or toys will be able to buy our children's self-worth. That comes from the love and time that they receive from us.

All the money we spend on our children today will be worthless to them in the future without the time and love from us to go with it now. Which is why the best currency for love is our time.

Us Time, the second part of the U URSELF Routine, is about quality and quantity, not either or.

It's about enjoying daily, dedicated time with our children and engaging with them in the present.

It's not about accomplishing anything or going anywhere special or doing anything in particular.

It's as much about the everyday moments we spend together as those planned special occasions.

Simply enjoying time with our children doing things such as reading a book together, visiting a local park, or even bathing them as part of their daily routines count as Us Time.

Us Time can be doing the most mundane, tedious tasks such as nappy changing, potty training, baths, and bedtime stories. These routines are often taken for granted and rushed or resented, but they can offer 'Quality Us Time' with our children.

It's at these times that bonds are strengthened. Suddenly, those boring mundane duties become opportunities to get to know each other better, to talk, laugh, cuddle, kiss, and appreciate each other.

We need to be able to switch off distractions to appreciate and enjoy them as such though. While changing their nappy for instance, we need to look around or listen to what is distracting us. If we find it's the TV on in the background competing for our attention, preventing us from communicating with our baby, we should switch it off.

Likewise, if we are going to give them a 'quick' bath, we should turn our phone off and have a 'quick' play in the bubbles with them.

Then we'll find ourselves engaging with our children in a more loving and meaningful way. This will make us want to spend more time together.

It's never about what we do as parents, it's how we do it, how we feel, and how our children feel as a result that matters.

Letting go of any end result and enjoying the process or journey with our children is what's important. And making sure our time together is happy and relaxed and that we look forward to it as much as our children do.

Three hours spent frustrated and bored doing homework about castles is not the kind of time together that anyone will look forward to. On the other hand, a couple of hours visiting a local castle would be.

Turning otherwise boring, mediocre chores or routines into enjoyable experiences benefits everyone. We don't have to grudgingly get things done, I'm sure none of us think we do that, but often, we are unaware of the signals we are unconsciously giving off when we have to do things we don't enjoy or want to do.

It's not about getting the project done perfectly either, or achieving full marks, winning the game, or going to a certain place with certain people at a certain time.

Us Time is not about obligation like another 'to do' on our 'list' that we must get ticked off. We don't want to get the time over and done with or do as much as we can in an allotted amount of time. The whole point of Us Time is having fun with our children, purely for the sake of having fun.

Once we have U time for ourselves, having fun with our children is not such a crazy notion. We'll feel more relaxed and content and an hour of dedicated Us Time a day becomes manageable when we make it a habit and schedule that time for that purpose.

And finding an hour of Us Time a day should be easy enough once we start practising saying 'no' to 'Time Takers.' The only issue is whether we want to spend an hour a day dedicated to our children?

If your child's behaviour can be difficult, this may not be something you relish doing, you may or may not be surprised to know that many parents have admitted openly to me that they actively look for distractions away from their children. And lots of parents feel a sense of relief when they drop their children to childcare or school or go to work. This is not because they don't love their children, quite the opposite, they really do love their children, they just don't understand their behaviour or how to manage it, making time together more like hard work than fun, and they don't want to upset their children or themselves any more than necessary. If that sounds familiar, then you may be interested in reading my other book *The Powerful Proactive Parent's Guide to Present Parenting* because when we can understand our children's behaviour better and they can understand us, Us Time becomes a more pleasurable experience.

As parents, we are always going to be busy, and finding time to dedicate to our children without distractions such as phones and computers or other people, is always going to be difficult. Yet again, the problem does not need more time, we simply need to be more present when we are with our children, and appreciate that time together.

None of us actually spend as much time with our children enjoying their company as we think. Even stay at home parents who spend all day in the company of their children switch off and end up Autopilot Parenting, so much, they rarely notice doing it.

Our children do notice though, and they do all they can to make us conscious by demanding our full attention any way they can.

This usually results in us telling them off.

THE CONFIDENT PARENT'S GUIDE TO RAISING
A HAPPY, HEALTHY & SUCCESSFUL CHILD

WHAT HAPPENED?

Surely none of us would have chosen to become parents in the first place, had we thought we would end up angry, frustrated, nagging, stressed out, sleep deprived, nervous wrecks?

We become parents with the sole intention of enjoying every moment with our children and to love, cherish, and appreciate the joy they bring.

Yes, before our beautiful bundles of joy arrived, we dreamed of picnics in the park, their little faces lighting up on Christmas day, their first steps. As we envisioned a beautifully decorated nursery where our new arrival would sleep like a baby, peacefully through the night, there were no negatives ever considered in our minds.

We never thought as far as the reality that most parents face such as, fussy eating, cleaning up after a sickness bug, never ending dirty nappies, sleepless nights tending to a miserable, screaming baby with colic, teething, bedwetting, nightmares, or the food encrusted carpets, sticky furniture surfaces, paint all over the walls, playdough over the floor's bombsite a toddler would create in our once beautiful homes.

And it's doubtful any of us could have imagined our little cherubs ever uttering the words 'I hate you' or fibbing to get their own way as we daydreamed of the first time they called us mum or said they loved us

But have our children let us down, or have we all just been naively seduced by the notion of what parenting should be like?

The truth is, parenting can be a joyous experience full of fun times together, but equally, we need to be prepared for the not so fun times too. Like any other relationship, it does take a lot of time and patience to build rewarding, loving relationships with our children.

It doesn't matter what parenting tools or techniques we use, or how much advice we receive from others, without enough time to devote to our children, it's all worthless and ineffective.

The good news, however, is the time and effort needed in Us Time is what will build those happy, healthy, and successful relationships with our children.

But we have to make the time for it.

TO DO OR NOT TO DO—STREAMLINING

Having too many things on our 'to do list' takes our time and attention away from our children.

We would certainly all be more effective and more relaxed parents if we did not juggle so many balls in the air.

There're only so many balls we can juggle at any one time, so we have to drop a few.

As our children are those closest to us, they're naturally more loving and forgiving than anyone or anything else in our life.

We can certainly put them off a lot easier than we can our job or our everyday chores. Sadly, for those reasons, they are the balls that get dropped first when we have our hands full.

Even when we are spending time with our children, all too often, we are occupied with thoughts of work or relationship issues or fretting about the future, instead of concentrating on them.

Understandably, with our busy schedules and hectic lifestyles, our minds can and do easily wander from the trivia of our children's conversations or complaints to our more pressing grown up issues.

We will all be more efficient and effective parents though if we learn how to streamline our commitments. For parenting to run smoothly, we have to be organised, but too many diaries, schedules, plans, and to do lists just keep us constantly busy. We don't want our arms to become so tired that we drop all the balls but that's inevitable over time when we are struggling with too many for too long.

Seeing in black and white everything everyone else wants us to do and how much has to be done can feel daunting. And putting a slot in our diaries for our children's 'Us Time' can easily get lost.

The less balls we have in the air, the more fun we can have with our children, so it's time to drop those 'Time Takers' once and for all.

Keeping one diary and one intention for the day; to be happy spending time doing what we love with those we love most, is all we really need.

That's in the ideal world anyway; in the everyday world that we have all created, we do things we dislike with those we don't particularly love because we have to. But we can get rid of the unnecessary or unwanted, then focus on the rest of the things we spend so much time planning to do, which can be done now, not tomorrow, next week, or next month.

THE BUSY-NESS DISEASE

The reason we make plans is because we are all so busy.

This current parenting epidemic known as the 'Busy-ness Disease' is causing our relationships to suffer, and it's the biggest obstacle to US Time.

But we have to have clarity on why we are busy all the time.

Who are we doing it all for anyway?

As parents, more than anything else, our children are the reason we go to work and do what we do, whether that's housework or paid employment.

We've seen how 'Time Takers' can rob us of our precious U Time, but we can also rob ourselves as well as our children of Us Time by making ourselves too busy.

EXTRACURRICULAR

Prioritising Us Time means we no longer resent or desire to delegate those mundane duties to others.

It's not that as parents we ever wanted to anyway, but we are all faced with trying to prove ourselves in a competitive world. Working our way up the career ladder, maintaining a social circle of friends, driving the newest car, or living in the right postcode area is keeping us away from Us Time with our children and causing the 'Busyness Disease'.

Although we feel we are doing it for our children, are they really benefitting from all our hard work?

If we are honest, the more we have, the more we want, so, will we ever have enough that we feel that we can relax and do less and spend more time playing with our children?

We happily embrace breakfast clubs and after school extracurricular activities these days, not only because they help us to do more for others, but we believe this way, our children are getting what they need.

The belief is that, if we don't provide our children with extracurricular activities or encourage them to study instead of play, they won't succeed in such a competitive world either. And so our jobs and those extracurricular activities through which our children attend end up taking up all of our free time together—our Us Time—is the one thing that ironically will benefit our children the most, both in the long- and short-term. Feeling unhurried, happy, understood, loved, secure, accepted, and worthy of our time is all our children want or need to grow up into happy, healthy, and successful adults. But that takes time.

It's time to get organised and do what we must and forget about the rest. Some things are pointless.

CLEANING IS CLUTTER

Knowing the importance of Us Time helps us to organize our time more effectively around our children's needs. Everything else in our life is pointless clutter, even the cleaning.

In my experience, dust never disappears, but our children's youth does.

There's always going to be laundry in the basket, dishes in the sink, and dust on the TV.

Quite simply, as long as we are alive, it never ends, so we needn't feel the housework has to be done before we spend time with our children. I know it's embarrassing when an unexpected visitor turns up and the house is a mess, but living life is more important than looking good to others. If those visitors are important in our lives, then they won't mind we prioritise spending time with our children over a tidy house sometimes.

Our children will not always need us like they do now, but the time we spend with them today will make a big difference that will stay with them for a lifetime, unlike that worn-out jumper that always needs washing and ironing. We can vacuum and polish until our heart's content when our children have grown up and flown the nest. Admittedly, we won't have as much mess then, but who will we be keeping the house clean and tidy for?

An empty house is just a house, not a home.

Our homes are our family space to feel safe, relax, and play in. Children need enough space for playing with their toys and belongings. Sometimes, games, puzzles, dolls, and figures need to be left out in order for them to pick up playing where they left off last. They don't want a Feng Shuied bedroom with books and toys neatly stored away like ornaments just to look at. That's just a waste of money. Useless, unused boxes of toys gathering dust just create more unnecessary cleaning. Toys that are loved and used often don't gather dust, only memories.

Tidying and cleaning is best done little and often each day. The more prepared and on top of things we are, the more time we have to enjoy with our children.

THE NIGHT BEFORE

Trying to iron school uniforms in the morning when we are running late is never a good option. To save time and stress, it's preferable to spare an hour when we're not busy to blast through the ironing pile in one go. We could even turn that time into bonus Us Time if we get our children to read their schoolbooks to us as we iron or watch a movie together at the same time.

Or consider paying someone else to do the ironing?

There're ironing services that pick up and drop off ironing at a reasonable price, and the time and stress they save more than make up for the cost. Mornings run so much smoother when we can reach in the wardrobe for fresh, clean, pressed clothes, and this is as important for our own outfits as much as our children's.

Deciding what everyone will wear the night before and laying out the school uniforms, PE kits, bags, shoes, homework, and making the lunches, or putting the dinner money in an envelope should help to alleviate the unnecessary morning panic and chaos.

First thing in the morning is the most important time of day as it sets the mood for the rest of the day. Trying to have everything done and ready the night before not only ensures a smoother, easier, more joyful start to the day, but increases the likelihood that the rest of the day will continue well.

LET'S DO IT NOW

We need to make a habit of dealing with things as soon as we can, instead of saving them for later.

This way, they won't all stack up to be an insurmountable mountain that we have no energy to tackle.

Let's check our diaries and to do lists today, and do all the things that can be done now.

If there's too much that can be done now, is all of it necessary? If not, can we get rid or delegate it?

Having to buy or make a costume for our children's school concert, for example, is much easier and far less stressful, if we tackle it the day we find out about it. I myself have all too often set the school letters aside and thought 'I will do that nearer the time, at the moment, there are more important things to do today.'

Then before I know it, the costume has to be taken into school the next day for the show, and I have no time or resources to make one and no time to shop around or get one delivered from the internet either.

In a mad, frantic rush around the shops, I discover no one even knows what an Okapi is, let alone sells the outfit or knows where I can get one, and I need to improvise.

Trust my Daughters costume to be an Okapi and to have a Horse's head, the neck of a Giraffe and the legs of a Zebra!

Even with time on my side, that required three different animal costumes. Suddenly, finding that outfit that appeared so unimportant last week, now becomes a full-on emergency.

The lesson in the story is; if we want to save ourselves a lot of time, money, and stress, we should never put off until tomorrow what we can do today, and not put off until tomorrow, what we can put off indefinitely.

DELEGATE CHORES NOT US TIME

When we are struggling to get everything done or find Us Time, we know we have taken on too much and need to learn to delegate to others.

Most people can do what we do, with the exception of being a parent to our child.

Sharing work with others and doing chores such as shopping online to save time parking and packing, can free up some extra Us Time.

Alternatively, we can include these things as part of Us Time. Children like to feel grown up and to do what grown-ups do. They enjoy sorting the clothes into colours, putting the washing machine on, and pegging the clothes on the line, so we can delegate them some responsibility. They will need to learn these skills one day, so they may as well get into the habit and start learning now, it's education, not exploitation.

When we include them, we are not multitasking them with chores if they are involved and enjoying the process, so let's get them involved.

The difference is the way in which the task is approached and how we treat them. Instead of our children competing with the vacuum cleaner for our attention while we scream and shout at them over the noise, we can involve them in what we are doing.

This way, we not only get help to complete chores, but have less stress and more fun time together. This 'Busy-ness Disease' is just as harmful as not being around for our children at all.

When we are visible but inaccessible to our children, it's like saying to them that they're lower down on our list of priorities or second best to whatever else has captured our attention.

While we are physically around them, they can actually see what is more important to us at that time other than them. Whether it's the housework, watching TV, or chatting on the phone to a friend, they know that at that moment, they are not as important to us as the thing or the person we are currently occupied with. We can use our U Time to chat with a friend, but our children shouldn't need an appointment to chat to us.

All these things that keep us busy seem important at the time, but it doesn't matter what we have or achieve in life—it's all a waste of time. It's who we are with and the time we give that counts in the end!

DUVET DAYS

There's a lot to be said for our children feeling under the weather, although we never want for them to be ill, it's one of the few times when we are dedicated and interested in their every need.

We drop everything just to be on hand for them, attentively watching their every move, listening to what they say about how they feel. Suddenly, we realise how precious they are to us, and how we really prefer it when they are loud, lively, and bouncing around us, as opposed to being quiet, still, and undemanding.

We ignore our busyness and stop trying to multitask our children with other things such as work, housework, partners, or TV, finding ourselves actually enjoying a Duvet Day, cuddled in together watching Disney DVDs and drinking Chicken Soup.

My own children who are older now, look back with fond memories of their sick days from school. Often, the one who was well would feel envious of the one who was home with Mum, lapping up all my time and attention. Like most other children, they didn't want to go back to school after all the time and attention they were comforted with while ill.

I understand that not every parent has the option of taking time off whenever their child is ill, and some children pick up illnesses more than others, meaning they can have a cough and cold most days. And even when our children are ill, our jobs still need doing, and we still need to earn money, making it hard to just relax or take time to tend to their every need.

I've also seen lots of unsympathetic employers put immense pressure on parents to get to work despite their children being ill. Understandably, they have their bottom line to think about, not our family affairs.

Yet, nothing or no one could need us more than our children.

One day, our little children will grow-up and leave home. We too will get older and eventually retire and leave that job.

But guaranteed, it won't be our ex-boss or our clients who will be coming to visit us, thanking us for all our hard work, nor will they be taking us out shopping or caring for us if we are ill either!

But if we need them, hopefully, our children will.

Us Time is about not waiting for our children to be ill before we enjoy a 'Duvet Day' together. It's about making them a regular part of Us Time, all of the time.

MAKE DAILY INDIVIDUAL US TIME FOR EACH CHILD

It's great to spend family 'Us Time' together, but trying to please more than one child at the same time can be difficult. Each will have different interests from the other, and will likely try to compete for individual attention, but being blessed with more than one child can make finding time for each one challenging.

Although generously giving of our time can become a stretch, each child will benefit from the attention of one on one time, making them feel special and important.

That's why it's important to factor in 'US Time' for each individual child by asking each one to write a list of the things they would like to do during US Time. One child may be a football fanatic but if your other child isn't, then taking them to football matches isn't going to be the time they will enjoy. Of course, there will be times when they will have to tag along, but this isn't what we class as 'Us Time'.

Family Us Time is still important, and finding things we all like to do is a lot easier when we have a list to look at and see where everyone's preferences lie so we can plan to do those things together, alongside individual Us Time.

SURPRISE & SPONTANAETY

When we are trying to cope with the demands of parenting in the beginning, we can get stuck in a rut. We like to do the same things as routine helps us to feel in control, or sometimes, we like to stay in and do nothing, as going out to unplanned places is too daunting to even think about. If we establish a routine in the important areas of our children's lives, then as part of our Us Time, we can afford to be spontaneous.

Nothing is more surprising than an unplanned outing, even if it's only a trip to the local park. Being in nature can blow away the cobwebs, helping us as much as our children to feel refreshed. It also strengthens the bonds we share, more so than an organised hour of footy in the park once a week ever could.

We can't make up for our absence with an hour here or there, or with gifts and treats. Short term, these may appeal to our children, but really, they are after our time and attention and will appreciate that more than anything else in the long run.

It was once thought that 'Quality' was more important than 'Quantity' but 'Quality Time' soon becomes convenient or planned time together. Now, this may sound contradictory as we have put Us time into our daily routine, setting aside time specifically for our children each day.

But the problem with that is, we may try to cram all our love and attention into that one hour or so, which defeats the object.

Parents who have access to their children only at certain times can't avoid this. But if we are fortunate to spend every day with our children, then we shouldn't be tempted to cram all our love, fun, time, and attention into one day, or worse, one hour with our children.

It's counterproductive spending a fabulous family Saturday together, cramming in all the love and fun we can into one day, if we neglect to do this on the other six days of the week.

This misses the whole point completely, as one day can never cancel out the other six days of the week, no matter how fantastic a day we've had with our children.

When we try to do this, our children end up overstimulated, tired, and often full up on junk food and unhealthy drinks. Leaving us worn out and skint by the end of the day, as we overcompensate by spoiling our children with treats out of guilt over all the time we are not spending with them on a daily basis.

Don't focus too much on the details such as what to do together and for how long, as this can turn Us Time into more of an inconvenience, especially if we can't agree with our children on what to do.

Every day presents spontaneous opportunities to have fun and enjoy time together with our children, so no need to make an appointment in our diaries to spend 'quality' time with our children or plan anything elaborate. Your child just loves being with you, no matter what you do.

It can be a good idea though to let them plan how you spend Us Time together sometimes. The planning of Us Time is a good activity in itself that can prolong and intensify the fun of time together. It's the planning and anticipation that our children will find the most exciting aspect, especially if they have the choice of where to go and what to do. It's like waiting for their Birthday to arrive, it's not about the gifts themselves that's exciting, but the anticipation of those gifts.

Also, planning future events together such as Birthday Parties can help us out too. Just as much as planning ahead, our children also love to look back on past fond memories with us. We can use Us Time to reminisce and revisit happy times in the past by going through old photos, videos, and mental memories together. Keeping the magic of those memories alive and evoking those good feelings we felt.

WHEN US TIME IS NO FUN FOR ANYONE

Disagreements at the beginning of the Us Time routine are commonplace. Don't feel disheartened if you disagree on what to do or fall out with your child in the middle of an activity or outing.

Just because it's Us Time and we've decided that we are going to make a real effort to get on with our children and spend more fun time together, doesn't mean we should expect them to feel the same way, they may need some time to catch up.

They will still misbehave as they would normally, although this can spoil Us Time together initially, it's just a teething phase that we should expect.

The best way to approach disagreements is to stay Present and Proactive, and be patient while reminding ourselves that our only aim is to enjoy spending time with our children.

US TIME IS PRECIOUS

Us Time is precious because, sadly, there will come a day when our children won't feel comfortable holding our hand in public, and they won't want to watch animated movies with us, and we might just miss or regret that.

If today was the only time, we had left on Planet Earth, chances are we would not want to clean our house or work overtime schmoozing our boss for a pay rise.

We would simply want to spend our time with our children and loved ones, having fun and letting them know how much we love them while appreciating how much we are loved by them also.

Our children won't always remember the specific dates or places or times we spent together with them, but they'll always remember how we made them feel. Let them only remember feeling loved and happy.

Childhood doesn't last forever, when our children reach their twenties, it's going to be too late to regret not having had the time to paint, play, cook, read, sing, dance, and enjoy our children while they were young, which is why the next part of the U URSELF Routine is all about Recreation and The Power of Play.

CHAPTER 5: RECREATION—THE POWER OF PLAY

PLAY IS PERFECT

MUCH I FIND IN the miracle of life is that life is perfect exactly as it is. Nature does its thing perfectly. From small acorns large oak trees do grow effortlessly, and they withstand all weathers and are flexible throughout as they bend and not break. Their roots are planted firmly in the ground, keeping them strong and steady and grounded. No one has to tell the tree to drop its leaves or change its many colours with the seasons. Even ants in an ant colony know their role in life, amazingly, our bodies can heal themselves, and we don't need to think about our bodily functions while we sleep it's all taken care of instinctively. And so it is with our children's learning in play, it happens naturally, when we let it.

What I've found recently is, children need to be occupied constantly. 'What's next? where next? I'm bored!' have sadly become everyday utterances of our young. And the ironic thing is, children today have more extracurricular activities, more toys and electronics, and more things than ever before. It's not things or experiences they are missing. The fact is, they have too much and too many things, constant stimulation, leaving peace of mind, relaxation, and true curiosity and play muted and hidden beneath a mass of worthless expense. They don't appreciate what they have, and all they see is what they perceive as missing and what they don't have. We are not helping our children by doing or buying more for them. We help them by making things special and teaching them gratitude.

It's not our children's fault that we keep filling their never-ending void with stuff they don't really want or need. It's ours. But why are we doing it?

To get them off our backs to stop them moaning and wanting?

Their needs and wants are insatiable, so we'll never accomplish that.

To stop us feeling guilty?

There's always something to feel guilty about, and if we are giving out of guilt, we are not addressing the real issue, which is usually our children wanting to be with us, and its time they crave not possessions.

If we fill their lives with extracurricular activities, we don't stop them being bored by constantly entertaining them, we teach them that their restlessness needs us to cater to it, and that's a never-ending cycle.

WHAT'S NEXT?

It's vital children have the chance to relax and unwind, this doesn't mean sleeping. Stimulation overload is a very real problem facing our children, affecting their mental health. Encouraging them to listen to relaxing music, read a book or comic, and take time to daydream is vital. Most children today see this as being bored, but there's a lot of benefits to boredom.

As parents, we are so busy in our own lives, we feel guilty when we are not providing busyness for our children, but what we all need and crave is time out from this busyness.

WEEKEND NEVER ENDS

One Monday morning, about twelve years ago, I remember asking a parent how her weekend had been, here's how she replied.

'Friday after school I took the children to football and gymnastics, then Saturday morning they had karate, and in the afternoon, I took them swimming at that new pool with all the big slides, but they got bored after half an hour so we ended up in the park. But they had worked up an appetite, so we went for a burger then on to the cinema. I think they are getting too old for animated films now though, as they soon got bored midway, and all they did was fight with one another then all evening. Then, you'll never guess what?'

I shook my head in disbelief thinking, What, there's more?

She continued, 'Sunday, I found out they had a big homework project that took most of the day up, I'm just so tired, I can't wait to get back to work today!'

Wow, wow, wow!

All that nonstop entertainment, time, and expense, and at the end of the day, none of it made them happy. What would, I wonder?

Too much can be just as bad as not enough. This conversation took place many years ago, but over the years, I find children are becoming a part of the 'What Next?' generation of dissatisfied children. An enjoyable picnic in the park is just never enough. Children seem to be asking their parents 'what's next?' before they have even finished doing what they are currently doing.

Leaving most of us worn out, skint, and frazzled by the end of the day.

The school summer holidays pose a real challenge for most of us, as we compile packed itineraries, lists, and mind maps of where to go and what to do to entertain their endless wants and desires.

As a child, I loved nothing more than our Sunday walk through the forest or hike up our local mountain. We did it every Sunday without fail, but my brother and I never bored of it, in fact, all week we looked forward to it.

Granted, we only had 3 TV channels back then when I was a child, where children's programmes were only aired for an hour at lunchtime. And we didn't have computers or phones then, so I never felt as though I was missing out on my screen time. Walking up a mountain or playing tag with the other children on our street was our entertainment, and we did it over and over again with the same enjoyment.

Often, I hear, 'It's boring, we've been here before,' when I take children out somewhere. As though every trip should be somewhere new and exciting. I fear Children are just losing their ability to entertain themselves and have fun naturally these days.

And children's play places are cashing in at our expense. When I was a child, a trip to the farm or zoo was a once a year treat, we were lucky to get a bag of sweets or a pencil or rubber from the gift shop at the end of our visit. Now, children expect expensive toys at the end of every day out. It's not our children's fault these venues strategically place the gift shop full of toys at the end of an attraction where we must walk our children through to leave. But the result is, as parents, we no longer feel a fun family day out is good enough when our children are clutching onto a fifty-pound toy, demanding they want it!

To add insult to injury, we know that we can get the same toy at half the price from the supermarket, but we also know all our children will remember is how horrible we were for denying them that toy, not all the fun we had having a picnic next to the peacocks! They are more interested in collecting things than collecting memories in our consumer driven exploited society. Luckily, for all these toy manufacturers and sales companies, we are all too busy to question their tactics aimed at us poor parents and our children, and none of us want our children to feel deprived. We just want our children to be happy!

I think what our children are really craving is that human, loving, connection, a kiss and a cuddle, a long hug and just being present together in the moment, not just there physically, but in mind and energy too. It's not their fault, they're not being ungrateful or selfish, they think that it's entertainment and more stuff that they need, but it's more loving 'Us Time' they are really seeking.

Life is about contrast, yin and yang, good with the bad, desire and fulfilment, indeed, one can't really appreciate the good times if there were no contrasting bad times or appreciate a treat if they get one every day. We'd have nothing to measure against, no anticipation or appreciation. Life can have lack at times but be appreciated more when what our children really want is then received. Life and relationships can be difficult, but equally, they can be great and rewarding too!

Daily U Time, as well as US Time is important, as it gives us permission to have fun and find out what we as individuals enjoy. For many, lack of time is not the issue though, we just don't know or have forgotten how to play properly, and sadly, so have our children.

PLAYING PROPERLY

Yet there's no right or wrong way to play, so relax, you can't get it wrong, neither can your child, but hey, they already know that.

If we find ourselves getting too serious when playing with our children or get angry whilst playing a game because they're not sticking to the rules and playing right, or frustrated it's taking too long, then we are not really playing at all.

When we try or it feels like hard work, then that's what it is, a chore, but if we enjoy ourselves and time flies, that's playing. Same for children too, if an activity feels like a task they must win, get right, or play it safe, they're not really playing.

They learn from losing and taking risks, and play offers them a safe haven to explore, learn, and fail. There's no right or wrong way to play, it's unstructured without rules or limits to the imagination.

Children inevitably learn through the process of play in their own way and time, so we can let them learn for themselves. Activities don't need to be productive and meaningful or have a specific learning outcome, they can just play for the fun of it and nothing else.

Children are more creative when left to use their own initiative. For a child, a game could have many outcomes and possibilities, where adults like sticking to the rules and finding the right or most logical way to win.

These adult led activities soon bore children as they usually have too many rigid rules that stifle creativity. Their goal is winning the game, as opposed to leisure fun. Some games need rules, but too many rules and structure can interfere with our children's enjoyment, learning potential, and progress. When my son was young, he played the game Connect Four on his own for hours, even though that defeated the object of the game. He was obsessed with dropping the coloured counters into the slots, making patterns that he would then watch come crashing out when he released them from the bottom. It wasn't the right way to play the game, but it provided hours of fun for my son, and I'm sure he learnt a lot about cause and effect.

Play is not about playing with a toy or game the right way; it's allowing our children to use their imagination, which rules only limit.

INTERFERENCE IN PLAY

Over the past sixteen years as a Childminder, I've had the opportunity to observe different age groups of children all playing together. At the beginning of my career, I felt the need to structure and plan activities and to keep them all busily occupied.

Now, experience has shown me that children require as little adult intervention as possible and more free choice and opportunities for spontaneous play.

This is when they have real fun and enjoy each other's company, and when you hear real laughter and joy.

When we interfere or try to entertain them constantly, they don't learn how to amuse themselves and inevitably get bored when left to their own devices. This can lead to negative or positive attention seeking behaviours.

Our children crave our time and attention, and delight in any we offer. They look to us for acceptance that they are doing it the right way. But we now know that when it comes to play, there is no right or wrong way, so we can encourage them to do it their way.

Even if they are technically wrong, we can allow them to think for themselves and show them that we don't mind. If they colour the grass purple when drawing a picture, then that's okay, it's their picture, we can approve of it exactly as they want it to be. The grass doesn't have to be greener!

There's a time and a place for formal learning and fact finding and a time and a place for freedom, love, and acceptance. Our children won't grow up believing the grass is purple because we haven't corrected them or criticised their picture when they were three years old. They'll soon learn it's green by themselves if given the opportunity to play outside. But they will grow up to feel creative, confident, and with a healthy level of self-esteem when we give them the freedom to express themselves in way's we don't think are correct.

ENGAGE & ADD INTEREST

Children ask for our input at times, but we don't need to give them our ideas, they have their own. We can be interested and question their ideas if it's appropriate, for instance, while doing a puzzle, they might ask if a piece goes in a certain place.

Instead of answering with 'yes' or 'no' we could say 'I don't know, what do you think, shall we try it and see?' and let them put the pieces together themselves.

They will learn more and have more fun when we are interested, curious, or helpful, but not too involved that we control or take over.

Finding ways to stretch an activity, as well as their imagination and concentration, is useful. Like suggesting they paint a treasure map with a story to go with it, while writing some clues to find hidden treasure for us to find that they make from junk materials, such as bottles and boxes or play dough. This can extend an activity and prolong their interest and creativity.

Sometimes, we can give our children too much choice, and this can overwhelm them. We may think that by giving them lots of toys or laying out different types of creativities to do that we are keeping them occupied, but this can have the opposite effect.

If we follow their every desire and whim, then no sooner than getting the paint brushes out, they will be onto the play-dough shouting 'Finished, what's next?' as they continuously flit from one activity to another, uncontentedly. Adding interest to an activity as in the above treasure map activity helps, but sometimes, we have to let them just get on with their own business of playing.

FREE PLAY

Their choice of what they want to play should be for them to freely choose. Playing is freedom. The side effect is often laughter.

Milestones and targets have worthwhile purposes, but play is spontaneous, we can't force it, it happens naturally, or at least it did. These days, children just don't know how to simply play or amuse themselves without technology. We have to go back to basics and allow our children the privilege of boredom so they can discover imaginative play again.

We can't do this if we keep providing things for them to do. They have to learn how to amuse themselves and become creative with nature.

Less is more when it comes to play, less intervention, and less toys, and more freedom and imagination is the way of free play.

This kind of Free Play is the core of our children's physical, mental, emotional, and spiritual well-being.

ONLY BORING PEOPLE GET BORED

There's not much left to the imagination anymore, and the absence of a TV, mobile phone, or computer can make our children feel bored. Unfortunately, being constantly occupied with people or electronic things prevents contemplation and creativity.

Children are so used to this type of stimulation, they cannot play alone or even with each other anymore, they just don't know how to occupy themselves without these props, so they say they are bored. I have an answer for that: 'Only boring people get bored.'

There's more for children to do today than any other time in history. There's so much choice, variety, toys, opportunities, and experiences, it's hard to believe that the word bored still exists in the English language.

Back in the Depression and Wartime days, children really did have nothing to play with, nowhere to go, and little to do, yet they never seemed to get bored like the children of today do. They had no other option, they had to amuse themselves, and they knew how to play and have fun naturally.

My children learnt early on never to utter those words 'I'm bored.' As soon as they did, they knew I would find them a list of things to occupy them, such as cleaning jobs or homework.

On hearing what I had to offer to alleviate their boredom, they suddenly remembered they had lots to be getting on with and got on with it!

Ironically, we help alleviate boredom by allowing them to become bored. This means occasionally removing toys and electronics. This is not a punishment, so to prove that to them, we have to join them in this practice too. This is probably something we will struggle with more than our children; I mean can you actually imagine a day without your phone, computer, or TV? We'd fall so behind on the soaps, social media, and junk email!

Boredom would eventually disappear, however, and our children would come to realise all there is naturally around them. They may struggle at first to find things to do, but given the alternative, such as cleaning their bedroom, they would soon find something to do which is more fun.

What could you be doing that's more fun instead?

JACK IN THE BOX

Play is a word usually associated with children. Adults work. Children play.

But the benefits of play are ageless, the only question is, can we remember as grown-ups how to play?

As a child, I had a toy called a 'Jack in the Box. I loved nothing more than watching as a clown like head popped out to startle me. Despite expecting it, each time, I always felt surprised and delighted. It was simply fun.

Where did that joy of something so simple disappear to?

Where has all the excitement and anticipation in life gone?

Have we grown up and forgotten how to play and have fun for funs sake!

Play encourages laughter, which is well known for its healing and anti-aging properties, a useful side effect for us grownups. And if we enjoy physically active play, it can help keep us fit and healthy. Even non-physical activities release chemicals in the body, such as endorphins, which reduce stress and tension. That's why I've included recreation (another grown up word for play) as part of the U URSELF Routine. It's another vital aspect because, when we take parenting too seriously, we miss out and deprive ourselves as much as our children of all the fun in life. Life is meant to be fun! If it doesn't feel that way to you at the moment, then you're not playing enough.

Indulging in frivolity when we are supposed to be working, however, can have negative connotations. Others may think we are immature or don't take our work seriously. But if we stressed less and had more fun in work, we'd take fewer sick days off and look forward to going to work each day, resulting in more productivity.

Children instinctively know how to play. They understand the benefits and enjoyment it brings, it's their main priority in life.

It was once ours too, so why did we stop playing and having fun?

As grown-ups, have we shut that box closed so tightly, that we are now more afraid of what may not pop out, than what will?

We are all capable of having fun, we just have to entertain the idea of opening that box and learning how to play again.

Was there something you once did or would like to do, such as playing a musical instrument, singing, painting, writing, crafts, tennis, martial arts, carpentry, or gardening?

GROW UP CHILDISH

Play keeps us happy, healthy, and looking and feeling younger, so growing up childish is a must, especially if we want to be able to communicate and understand our children more.

Recreational Play is powerful, not only in enhancing the bonds we share, but in contributing to our children's happiness, health, and development.

Play helps them to:

- Develop mentally, physically, socially, and emotionally.
- Express themselves.
- Be creative and imaginative.
- Safely experiment and explore new ideas and concepts.
- Process thoughts, feelings, and ideas.
- Resolve past issues.
- Relax.
- Concentrate.
- Communicate.
- Relieve anxieties and fears.
- Stay fit & healthy.
- Socialise.
- Learn.

WHAT IS RECREATION?

The word Recreation means to recreate, and we can do that as much as children love to, actually, we're re-creating our lives every day, but we are often unaware that we are doing so. Sometimes, this means we create experiences that are not always fun or just humdrum. But if we can create the boring unwanted stuff, then it stands to reason we can also create more fun in our lives too.

Children are master creators with vivid, unlimited imaginations that allow them to become anything and anyone, from a random object such as a chair to an Alien from Outer Space, nothing is off limits in their play.

It's this natural ability to shut off reality and enter play that offers them an essential form of escapism. A safe haven from stress, anxiety, and worry. Helping them to make sense of events and the world they live in, and to digest and learn new concepts at their own pace.

Recreation can be called many things, such as leisure, hobby, pastime, exercise, play, activity, amusement, sport, even work!

But play never actually feels like hard work.

How we feel and our concept of time, is how we can differentiate real play, from any other experience.

Play has the ability to immerse and stimulate to the point we lose track of all time and reality. Play throws caution to the wind and allows anyone at any time, to do anything, no matter how silly or unconventional.

Regardless of what we do with our children, if we are having fun, then we're playing. It's not the activity that counts, it's how we feel when we do it.

Genuine play always feels good as it replaces control for freedom, anxiety for laughter, and learning for entertainment.

GROW UP

Sadly, 'Grow up!' or 'Play properly' has been the message we have received from others all our lives. Although, our parents and teachers probably never allowed us to really do so. When grownups say play properly, what they really mean is 'play by the rules', or often, 'behave'. But play has no rules; it's about acting without restraints and using imagination and creativity. It's stepping out of the expected, something children do naturally.

When we've been told by authority figures we should grow up and stop acting so childish, they were wrong, children are meant to be childish.

No one has ever made it the law that once we reach a certain age, we should stop having fun and lead a serious life. Those beliefs are our own self -imposed restraints that we have been conditioned into believing.

We are all free to have fun and stay young as long as we can.

PLAYTIME

Our own childhoods can hold the key to having fun again. What did you once love to play or do?

Can't remember your favourite childhood past times?

Don't worry, you can have fun finding new ones.

Even turning our jobs, relationships, or exercise regimes into playful activities can make a typical day more fun and extraordinary.

This may require some imagination as we pretend we are a celebrity chef cooking dinner or imagine while having a candlelit bath we are at a luxury spa, but that's what play is all about.

We can be anything or anyone, limited only by our imaginations as we lighten up and play with possibilities.

We don't have to rationalise what we do or try to work other people out. If we just play with the concept that everyone else is just playing the game like us, because really, they are.

We all create our own reality and lives from our imaginations, it's up to us whether we choose to be serious or have fun in our daily lives.

IMAGINATIVE CREATIVE PLAY

Imagine playing more and working less in life?

Most people work at making things from other people's playful ideas and imagination. Artists, inventors, writers, actors, musicians, singers, carpenters, builders, etc. Even those in caring professions play and have fun.

Happy workers spread their joy to others, they never work a day in their life because they enjoy what they do.

Creativity and inventions come from playing with the imagination first, not observing something that already exists.

As adults, we need to unlearn a lot of what we've learnt in order to play. Luckily, our children can teach us how to play with possibilities that are different from the norm. As long as we are not tempted to dismiss their wild ideas or vivid imaginations as pointless fantasy, our children can become the creators of great new inventions in the future.

We can encourage them to become innovative by giving them Lego, junk materials, art and crafts, and play-dough. These teach about changing concepts and properties, allowing originality to flourish.

Also, providing time, space, and props to use in roleplay with real or imaginary friends, such as dolls, cars, little people or action figures, old clothing or household items like old telephones, we help to spark their imagination too. Children fall into roleplay like reality, which is useful in helping them to understand how others may think and feel and make sense of the world.

Playing with others also teaches them to socialise, share, and sort their differences out, as well as establish their own roles within a group and find their own strengths and weaknesses.

That's why imaginative free play is not to be underestimated or shunned in favour of more structured play but encouraged as the main vehicle for our children's learning.

STRUCTURED PLAY

There is a place for structured play, however (structured play, which is more organized and adult led, usually has specific objectives behind it), if delivered in the right way. Teachers in school and childcare providers such as child-minders are trained and experienced at delivering this type of play without children noticing they're being taught.

As parents though, this type of play is a lot harder to engage in or keep fun. When our children don't play the right way or try hard enough, it's easy for us to get frustrated with them. It can also mean setting aside a specific amount of time to complete a task. Children don't enjoy this kind of structured, rushed, or rigid type of play, particularly if the purpose is to learn something. They see what we are trying to achieve, and in their eyes, this means spoiling their fun.

Yet, structured play such as board games can not only provide our children with hours of fun and entertainment, but can teach valuable skills such as cooperation, turn taking, strategies, rules, reading, and counting. But unless we have a lot of time and patience, are open minded of outcomes, and are creative and imaginative ourselves, it's best to stick to free play until we re-learn how to play properly again, as we did as children.

LEARNING AND PLAY

Our children are constantly learning something new every day, and they learn and generate new ideas through playing.

Their seemingly silly games actually teach them so much about the world they live in. Although education and play seem like separate activities in their own right, they are actually one and the same, children cannot do one without the other.

To be effective learners, they need to know how to make learning an enjoyable experience, and when they play, they cannot help but learn something new.

Learning and Recreation are intrinsically linked. Defining the two is difficult, yet, often, there's a separate time and place for learning and play, such as the classroom for learning and the schoolyard for playing.

If we could only combine the two in all they do and offer them the choice about what they do based on their interests, play and learning would become a more enjoyable experience.

I believe radically reforming our Education System and the way our children are taught by scrapping subjects in favour of topics instead and using cross-subject learning, such as that introduced in Finland, would produce a more successful education system and improve league tables for literacy and numeracy. Using our children's obsession for computer games could also be a useful vehicle for playful learning if more games had playful learning objectives embedded in them, and were offered at home and in schools. Then children would look forward to going to school more and have fun achieving their full potential in life.

GETTING DOWN WITH THE CHILDREN

We learn how not to play as we age, so for this part of the U URSELF Routine, we can watch our children having fun and remember how it's done. For this, we need to be on their level, not just metaphorically speaking but physically too. Being close and getting down on the floor with them to play, watch TV, read, or have a chat helps them to feel we are really interested and getting involved. They can also see and reach us better this way.

We need to experience life and see things as they do to understand them.

We can start by copying the way they sit. Instead of telling them to sit properly, for a change, we can copy their varying seating positions and postures, such as hanging with our head upside down off the end of the sofa, legs in the air, while the blood rushes to our face.

This may sound silly or uncomfortable, because usually there are only a couple of seating positions as adults we adopt, such as slouching on the sofa. Yet all those strange positions that our children feel comfortable in, we used to find comfortable too.

If we try them again, we may find some of them more comfortable than our conventional way of sitting today!

Hard, carpeted, rubber, vinyl, concrete, wooden floors. Grassy fields, muddy banks, gravel pathways, steps, sandy beaches. Trees and a hundred and one other surfaces we used to sit on as a child didn't bother us in the slightest.

Every chair and bed were comfortable, and we had various ways of sitting, standing, laying, or bouncing on them. Somehow, though, as we grew up, only the best memory foam mattress would do, and the most expensive sofas and chairs, as long as we sit on them properly that is.

But children are comfortable anywhere and everywhere, no matter what the surface, quality, fabric, or right seating position may be.

- Just for fun today, copy your child's different postures and seating positions and try to recall some of your own old childhood ones. Have fun experimenting and making up some new ones together. This is one of the quickest ways to feel young, free, and liberated again.

PROVIDING PLAY SPACE OPPORTUNITIES

Hanging out with our children outdoors has the added benefit of fresh air and space. It doesn't have to be about going anywhere in particular or cost much money. Building a den or turning the garden into a paradise full of flowers can give our children their own secret garden hideout. And finance and space permitting, a small allotment can house an abundance of fruit and vegetables, providing hours of pruning, picking, and planting.

Most children would rather spend after school playing in the garden at home or going to the park or having tea at a friend's house, than attending afterschool clubs and classes or going to an indoor moneymaking venue anyway. That's the impression I've gotten looking after so many children after school.

A CHEAPER WAY TO PLAY

Children can have just as much fun doing a treasure hunt in the garden, having picnics in the park, or playing with a cardboard box than they do with a computer. They have to be given these opportunities and experiences though.

Toys today are designed to do everything so our children don't have to think. Dolls now talk, wee, eat, and cry, cars and trains move by themselves powered by batteries, electricity, and computers, nothing is left to imagination anymore. Even books are replaced by DVDs and e-book readers, so there's no need to imagine how characters look or even read the words on the page with audio books. Everything is already done for them, but is this better for our children?

Despite play being more hi-tech today, children still love playing with cardboard boxes more than the gifts themselves. Mine even used to fight over who had the biggest piece of bubble wrap to burst. Whatever expensive gifts came in those boxes were secondary to all the fun had with the packaging. One year, after spending hundreds of pounds on a new TV and various computer games and toys for our son, he spent all Christmas playing with a small eight-pound box of Lego that was a stocking filler!

Children do not understand the cost of the gifts themselves; they value things on the value that they have to them entertainment wise, not the cost those things have to us financially. If we can remember this before their next Birthday, then we'll save ourselves a small fortune.

Our children are overwhelmed and tired with everything, all they want is time out to relax and do what they want to do. Even time to socialise with friends is scarce these days as we are too afraid to let our children play out with friends, preferring the safety of virtual or remote friendships that happen over a computer. But is it really safer, and are these real friendships?

We are also more focused on achievement these days and tend to pay for organised activities such as sports clubs or music lessons, as opposed to letting them play out with friends. But is this what our children want or need?

Although providing our children with extracurricular activities, equipment, and resources is helpful, we do not need to plan their every minute of every day. They don't need an array of creativities, expensive toys, computers, or day trips out with detailed itineraries. A spontaneous walk in the woods is just as good as any day out. Children, if left to their own devices and imaginations, can find adventure anywhere.

LESS IS MORE

We can save ourselves money, time, stress and energy when we fight our urges to indulge them in things they don't need or want. Doing so also helps them to value and appreciate those things that they do have more.

But creating their own little playground in the garden with a trampoline, playhouse, swing or slide, can give them that opportunity for freedom, exercise, and adventure.

EXERCISE—A HEALTHY MIND IN A HEALTHY BODY

Children are naturally energetic; their bodies are meant to move. Even babies in the womb are active. Sadly, in our fear-based society, fewer children are going outdoors, getting the physical exercise their bodies need. We've succumbed to technology because we feel it's safer letting our children play with friends online rather than outside.

SOCIALLY ACCEPTABLE

Children no longer need to physically meet friends to interact, now they connect and communicate through technology. And although we don't want to enrol our children into organised activities every day and miss our

Us Time together, a couple of times a week, it's socially better, healthier, and often safer, to enrol our children in some sporting activity than leave them to their own devices in front of a screen.

This gives them the opportunity to exercise whilst meeting other likeminded children with the same interests as them, offering a sense of belonging by spending time with others, especially in team sports such as football.

Those involved in sports have the chance to socialise and make friends which improves their mental, social, and emotional health.

Forming relationships and improving social skills aside, sporting activities can also teach valuable lessons in cooperation, sharing, turn taking, and even how to deal with losing and conflict.

This makes making friends and conversation easier, and more interesting, as well as helping them to feel part of a group. And with team players comes opposition and competition, which is not always a bad thing either.

MOVING, MOVING

Exercise is important to everyone's emotional as well as physical wellbeing. As the Latin quote states, 'A healthy mind in a healthy body – Mens Sana in corpore sano.'

The benefits of exercise on our children are numerous, helping them to:

- Eat and maintain a healthy appetite
- Lose weight
- Boost memory and concentration
- Sleep
- Relax
- Learn
- Behave better.
- Enhance their moods
- Increase energy levels

- Fight against infections
- Increases self-confidence & self-image

Exercise releases endorphins, these are natural, happy, chemicals which can make children feel good and boost their mood.

Exercise can also change body shape, making children fitter, leaner, and toned, helping to boost their body image and physical confidence. This can reduce or prevent depression or anxiety.

Exercise also encourages them to socialize and make friends more, increasing their self-confidence and self-esteem further.

Even if our children are fit, well, eating, sleeping, and feeling good, they still need exercise to maintain their health, happiness, and success. Whether they feel happy, sad, angry, frustrated, or lack concentration, we need no excuse to get them doing some physical activity.

NO MORE EXCUSES

Exercise doesn't need to be a planned particular activity though; exercise is simply another word for movement.

Encouraging exercise shouldn't be costly or hard work. If we have six children all wanting Karate lessons, that could get costly!

It should be fun, free, and easy.

Not all children enjoy sports, so it's important to find activities they do like, such as gardening. This way, they'll be unaware of the energy they are using whilst sowing and digging as they become absorbed in the activity itself.

It doesn't mean spending lots of money on expensive gym or club memberships or forcing them to join the School Netball Team. Exercise is just another word for play time. The only thing that matters is they are moving their bodies.

That could mean playing with friends, going to the park or indoor soft play area, kicking a ball about in the garden, playing tag, hopscotch, riding their bikes, skates or scooter. Simply playing, walking, running, skipping, jumping, hopping, or bouncing on a Trampoline are all fun ways for children to keep fit and active.

Most young children love to play actively. It comes naturally to them. A quiet child who sits silently in front of a screen is not so natural.

But fear not, this is a growing trend, and if your young child prefers screen time to physical play, it could be down to their comfortable habit of inactivity or obsession.

Children can easily and quickly become addicted to computer games or TV. Programmes are designed to be attractive and addictive.

We can't prevent our children from doing what every other child their age is doing, but we can monitor what they do and encourage them to do other things alongside.

Regular outdoor breaks and movement should be encouraged, they won't be able to regulate this themselves as they'll be hypnotised by a screen, so we need to get them up and moving and motivated again.

This can be hard for us to do if we are not active ourselves, but we will be teaching them a valuable lesson in self-care and respect if we can exercise and motivate them to.

This will stand them in good stead, not only as children, but later on as adults too. Statistically, the chances are if they stay inactive now while young, they will grow up into inactive adults.

Taking regular daily exercise today will benefit them later on, setting them up with healthy habits for the future.

We create their habits by making the rules and routines for them to follow. Making exercise a daily part of their routine encourages the habit of exercise.

If they've been accustomed to munching snacks in front of a screen, they might think this makes them happy and see no wrong in what they are doing, but as responsible, Proactive Parents, we know it's not good for them, and we have to demonstrate a better way. We have to get up and get moving ourselves and stop them doing those unhealthy things.

Excuses, such as lack of time, too much to do, or too tired are the enemies of exercise. We would get more done, quicker, with more vigour if we made a habit of exercising daily. In fact, the best time to exercise is when tired, as energy creates energy. The more active we become, the more energy we will have.

Some children are sportier than others and love any physical activity. Others are not competitive by nature and resist exercise, but that shouldn't stop them from being active in other ways, like walking the dog.

Sometimes, children hold self-limiting beliefs about their abilities such as:

'I'm too big to be a gymnast.'

'Too short to play basketball.'

'Too slow to run a marathon.'

'Too uncoordinated to play tennis.'

Yet everyone can still partake in these activities regardless. When they do, they realise those beliefs they hold aren't true or at least are not a barrier to doing them for fun. Everyone has something they are good at, so it's just finding that thing that your child does enjoy. That doesn't mean they have to be good at it though, there's a difference between enjoying something and competing to be the best. When encouraging our children to exercise and have fun—go for the joy, 'it's the fun, not winning, that counts!'

I've known many a child who is fiercely competitive and wins at everything. Particularly excelling in a sporting endeavour, but few if any who enjoy it.

On the other end of the scale, I've known children who lack energy and motivation in everyday tasks. They need exercise more than most, even though they think they don't. Children shouldn't be tired; they're meant to be carefree and energetic.

So, no more excuses, get them up and get them going, or maybe it's us who need motivating to move?

Maybe your child could encourage you to lead a healthier more active lifestyle?

My daughter persuaded me to take part in Race for Life; a charity run raising money for Cancer Research.

We bought a Treadmill for the house and went running around our neighbourhood two evenings a week. We all loved the US TIME spent together while getting daily exercise in the process. All for a good cause, benefitting us as much as the charity. Running was an activity we could all do whatever the weather too, indoors when the weather was bad, outdoors when it was fine, so there was no excuse.

HABITUALLY HEALTHY

If we let children develop their own habits, they will. Meaning they end up constantly sat at the computer or TV, not getting the exercise their bodies need to function effectively.

As children grow up, if they are not used to exercising, it'll take time to acquire the habit. If they are unfit or overweight, this can be difficult to begin.

So, let's begin now. As proactive, loving parents, we wouldn't let our children go a day without sleeping, eating, or even brushing their teeth, because even something as trivial as brushing their teeth has an effect on their health and how they look. For most children, brushing their teeth is second nature, it's a habit they do automatically because they have done it over and over again, so many times.

Some need a little nagging to do so and checking on. It's the same for exercise, it should become a habitual way of being for our children, not an activity to be done now and then when they feel like it. Sometimes, they will need us behind them nagging and checking on them in the same way we would be about brushing their teeth.

Children need to exercise physically, such as swimming, as well as mentally, such as reading. We don't need to get obsessive though, most children get their exercise naturally every day. They don't need to do athletics to be physically fit, or sit at a desk studying mathematics to be mentally stimulated. Everyday life presents them with these opportunities. Turning exercise into an everyday fun activity will help form habits our children look forward to. Once they find something they enjoy doing, it'll be hard to stop them, and they'll automatically form a routine keeping them habitually, healthy and happy.

Classes and team sports have their advantages, but they don't have to attend a formal class or lessons, although they do form an easy habit to follow. However, the restrictiveness or strictness of a lesson type exercise can soon become uninteresting and boring to children, especially if they have to wait to take turns or there is a desired learning outcome.

When we've invested in classes or bought the kit for our children, our desire to want them to excel can overtake the point of what we are trying to achieve. Exercise is about expending some energy. Fun's the secret component to creating the habit of exercise, not them thinking it's something they must or need to do or achieve in order to please us or make anyone else feel proud.

BREAK TIME IS BRAIN TIME

Once they start school, much of their time will be spent indoors in a classroom. No wonder they are like a bottle of pop ready to explode when we pick them up at the end of the day. All that pent-up energy needs releasing. Traditional playground games such as tag, hopscotch, and skipping are all fun and energetic ways to get their daily exercise. If they are not engaging in these playground games and running about freely, then what are they doing at school break time?

Hopefully not sitting down snacking.

We can chat with them and find out how they spend their break times and about the advantages of moving their bodies, playing physical games, and keeping active as much as possible.

Exercise benefits body and mind, increasing blood flow to the muscles and the brain, improving intelligence and impacting their learning capabilities, increasing brain activity and its size.

Neuroscience proves exercise is good for the brain and that active children have better memories, and their minds are more alert after exercise, creating new neural connections and increasing the number of neurons [brain cells] essential to digest more information and for our children's future development.

Therefore, children who exercise learn and concentrate better at school as well as improve their memory and general health. Intellectual advantages aside, there are many wealthy, happy, and very successful people who have left school with no qualifications, but they all needed one thing to achieve their potential in life, their physical health.

If they are sat down at a desk in school all day, they won't have the chance to expend all their energy, so we need to encourage them to be active whenever they can.

If we struggle to wean them off the TV or Computer, then we can try this bargaining technique called the 'Bursts of Fitness 15 Minute Rule'

THE BURSTS OF FITNESS 15 MINUTE RULE

The rule is, for every fifteen minutes of sedentary play, i.e. screen time with either TV or computer they engage in, then then have to take a short break to run up and down the stairs/garden/hallway or wherever is suitable and convenient. They must do this fifteen times before they resume their sedentary pastime for another fifteen minutes.

This is repeated every fifteen minutes. If they start off watching TV, they end on a run, if they start on a run, they end on watching TV. These fifteen-minute bursts of fitness breaks over the course of an hour of TV could add up to sixty runs up and down the stairs, which, depending on how many stairs we have, could be at least half of their hour, if not almost an hour of their recommended daily exercise. In this way, they get the best of both worlds: exercise and relaxation, and both at the same time.

This exercise is not a punishment, so there's no need to ban TV or Computers. As long as they're receiving their daily quota of exercise.

If they are active throughout the day or they attend sporting activities, depriving them of some quiet time to watch TV or play a computer game isn't necessary. So, for very active children, this exercise is not required, it's aimed at potential couch potatoes in the making.

There has to be a balance, if we want to create habitually, healthy habits long-term. It's a bit like going on a strict low-calorie diet that isn't necessary. If we keep depriving ourselves, we'll get fed up and bored and end up binging on excess calories.

HOW MUCH IS ENOUGH?

If your child appears bored, frustrated, fidgety, or seems lethargic much of the time, then there's a good chance they are not getting enough exercise.

It's never too soon to make exercise a habit, in fact, the earlier the better.

We can start from birth by letting babies kick about on the changing mat, then when they are a couple of months old, placing objects just out of their reach, encouraging them to stretch and reach out to grab them.

Also allowing Tummy Time where they can safely lay on their tummies and move about lifting their head and stretching out.

Once crawling, we need to allow plenty of space in a safe environment to crawl or roll around.

If under five years, they will need at least three hours of physical activity including indoors and outdoors every-day. But don't worry, under-fives are busy bees and will get most, if not all, of their exercise through playing.

We can just let them get on with doing what they do best, running around playing, as this keeps them flexible and encourages growth and development, reducing the risks of poor health.

At this age, they need no encouragement from us to be active. As long as they are getting a good mix of light activity, such as standing up, walking, stretching and rolling, alongside energetic physical exercise such as riding a trike or chasing a ball, totalling three hours a day, they'll be happy and healthy. I like to get the children huffing and puffing, dancing to action songs in the morning, this is when they should have most of their energy after a good night's sleep. Then they have free play with toys of their choosing, then lunch, some children nap, then out to the park or soft-play for an hour or so when they get their second wind, then the school runs, then drawing, painting or playdough, refuel at tea time, followed by TV, puzzles, or story time.

Don't even attempt to take your little one to the park, or soft play area to get their three hours all in one go. They'll be exhausted after an hour or so of running around, and you'll end up with a banging head.

To ensure a balance, we need to evenly space the three hours of exercise throughout the day, allowing for regular rest and nap times in between physical activity.

Children aged five to sixteen need at least an hour of exercise every day. To be healthy, they need to include aerobic, as well as bone and muscle strengthening activity into that hour. Muscle strengthening exercise will require some resistance or weight lifting, not using dumbbells but by supporting and lifting their own weight, such as climbing up ropes or climbing frames, hanging from trees or doing gymnastics or tennis. Bone strengthening is the same as muscle strengthening by lifting their own weight or going against some resistance and climbing on monkey bars or frames, but also by skipping, walking, jumping, hopping, running, martial arts, dancing, aerobics, or swimming.

Gymnastics, running, football, rugby, or martial arts, to name but a few, will help our children to get their recommended amount of all three aerobic, bone, and muscle strengthening exercise.

However, they don't need to do all their hour on one activity. It's far easier for them to break it up using their breaks and lunchtime at school. Which should contribute if not add up to one hour throughout the day of free time to exercise. But they will need to be running around active, not sat in choir practice for it to count.

WHAT COUNTS AS EXERCISE?

We've pretty much covered what counts as an exercise by now, it's anything that gets them moving. And anything that gets their hearts pumping causing them to work up a sweat is best.

And best of all, it can be free and does not have to cost a penny. Walking to and from school is a great way to start and finish each day. And housework such as tidying their bedroom helps us as well as them.

All exercise will help them to stabilise and maintain weight or burn off calories, and develop and improve their muscles, coordination, stamina, and balance.

The following suggestions can help motivate and encourage children to get involved and stay dedicated to regular exercise, and they are fun to do together as part of Us Time if we can remember that exercise needs to be a bit of:

- A challenge
- Fun
- Fresh air and adventure
- A boogie

A BIT OF A CHALLENGE

I'll never forget when my daughter was younger and the time she went bowling with friends.

She was doing extremely well, winning all the games, I was so proud of her.

Yet while I was congratulating her on winning the final game, I noticed she seemed unimpressed with herself:

'Aren't you happy you won?' I asked.

She replied, 'Well, the first time I won, I was really excited. But when you keep winning, it gets boring after a while, after the second and third time, it's just 'uh I won again.'

Any activity that becomes boring won't interest or engage children for long. There has to be a bit of a challenge involved or some healthy competition.

HEALTHY COMPETITION

Competition keeps things exciting and can help children to problem solve, strategize, and develop leadership skills.

Even team players need to play against other teams and to compete. This is necessary because the object of the game would be defeated if the goalie stood away from the goal to let the other team score in order for both teams to have the same scores and be winners.

It would be such a boring game, there would be little point in playing it. It's the competition and trying to win that makes the game fun in the first place.

This type of healthy competition encourages children to try harder, achieve more, and to motivate and push themselves further.

However, if a child is not competitive by nature, and they shy away from competition, then on occasions such as School Sports Day, emphasis should be on taking part, not on winning. Every child should feel included and be encouraged to participate without pressure or the burden of coming first.

Emphasis should be placed on enjoying themselves and trying their best, not, try their best to win.

As with any endeavour, it's not about the activity or goal itself that's so important, it's how our children feel in the process of taking part in an activity or working toward a goal.

In such an ever increasing, competitive society, it's easy to lose sight of our goals as parents and the objectives we want our children to achieve. We want them to win to feel good about themselves, of course, but if they lose, we don't want them to feel bad or less than. Placing emphasis on winning or reaching goals over feelings and being in the moment is counterproductive, yet, losing is no fun either but sometimes necessary.

In real life, our children won't be good or win at everything. Sheltering them from failure won't help them deal with defeat. But healthy competition can improve resilience to losing.

I've witnessed children who train to win, and most of the time they do, but they never enjoy that moment. The moment that sticks with them and hurts them the most, is the one time they fail or lose. It hits them hard; they're not used to it; they get sour grapes. They find excuses such as they didn't feel well or the other person must have cheated. They just don't like sharing in others' success, which unfortunately means, others are not so keen in congratulating them in theirs.

Most children who do what they do because they genuinely love doing it, means having a talent at sport brings out their confidence in their abilities, allowing them to shine. Competitive exercise can even benefit a shy or withdrawn child if they lack confidence in other areas of their life.

Sport is a competitive game, but competing can encourage introverted children to come out of their shells and explore. Combat sport where they have to spar against an opponent or learn to defend themselves can build self-confidence. And mastering or achieving belts or trophies does wonders for a child's self-esteem.

Shy children should not avoid sport because it's too competitive, but embrace it as it can help increase their confidence.

Whatever type of child, if they succeed or achieve in a chosen form of exercise, without feeling forced or pressured, or if they are relied upon in their roles, such as the football goalie saving goals or the goal scorer helping their team to win, this increases their confidence and self-worth.

The positive perception that they have of themselves, and the way their teammates congratulate and view them increases their self-esteem, improving their overall self -image. They may feel like they are a failure academically, but that won't bother them if they realise their physical strengths and worth.

If our children are in the habit of regular exercise, this taking care of themselves will be reflected in how they think and feel about themselves. And the fitter they are, the better they will be at exercise and certain sports.

Their confidence will grow the better they become, but by exercising and burning off calories, they will also look fitter, slimmer, and be stronger.

It's this looking good that creates a healthy self-image as they grow and develop, which becomes more significant the older and more self-aware they become.

A BIT OF FUN

Keep it fresh and fun. If they have a fear of water and hate getting wet or are body conscious, then swimming may not be fun for them. Although avoiding swimming completely would be unhelpful, as the more they face their fears the more chance of overcoming those fears and less hang ups they will have. But here, for the sake of encouraging exercise, it's best to start off with things they enjoy doing over those they don't.

Most children find bouncing on a Trampoline fun, they find it amusing falling all over the place as they laugh themselves fit. It's a great form of exercise that can be done independently or with others, and bouncing about in fresh air has to be good.

It's good for:

- Developing motor skills.
- Coordination between brain and muscle and gross motor skills because it uses large muscles in the body.
- Firming, toning, and increasing muscle strength,
- Metabolism,
- Confidence,
- Balance,
- Circulation.
- Strengthening heart muscles and body cells.
- Lowering cholesterol levels.
- Increasing resistance to disease.
- Improving oxygen supply.
- Increasing pulse rate.
- Energy and vitality.

Due to the strenuous nature of trampolining and the repetitive jumping action, children are able to improve and build up their bones, all with a low joint impact. While the Trampoline pad absorbs the impact of landing, strengthening and protecting bones and joints. It can even increase their appetite as it increases metabolic rate and helps to process nutrients effectively, helping to maintain and keep weight down. As it requires them to go against gravity, it's a great weight bearing exercise too. But here's the fun bit, trampolining also helps release those positive, mood enhancing chemicals known as endorphins, which help our children to feel happier.

But as already said, I like to dance with the children. It's so much fun, it doesn't feel like exercise at all.

A BIT OF A BOOGIE

Children need to raise their heart rate so they're breathing fast and hard. Walking is good for moderate activity, but they need more vigorous, intense, aerobic exercise, such as running or dancing too.

For younger children, Musical Playtime is a great way to get them dancing. Put on some action song classics, such as 'Head, Shoulders, Knees and Toes' and join in doing the actions with them.

Not only will they have fun learning the parts of the body, but they'll get some aerobic exercise in the process.

Dancing to the music channel on TV or the radio is a good way to encourage older children to get up and get moving. Allow them to pump up the volume and join in with them too.

Even if they only burn calories laughing at our dance moves, by making it fun and enjoyable, it's an activity that's more likely to become a habit they do more often.

A BIT OF FRESH AIR

We all need a bit of daily fresh air, but by simply taking our children out for a walk in nature, we offer them an adventure. From bug hunting to blackberry picking, adventures don't feel like exercise but fun.

Taking them out in all weathers, wet, windy, snowy, or sunny conditions will encourage or rekindle a love of the elements. This way, their surroundings become an opportunity to explore, rather than an exercise or inconvenience.

Whatever the weather, there's no excuse not to go outside.

'There's no bad weather, only bad clothes!'

As long as they've got a raincoat and wellies, jumping in muddy puddles will be all the exercise they need.

No need to worry about catching a cold, there's more chance of them getting ill from being cooped up in a stuffy room with the heating on watching TV. Instead of wrapping them up on the sofa in a blanket, take them out for a breath of fresh air. Being outside and exercising boosts immunity and can aid recovery when children are ill.

Being in touch with nature is said to be more beneficial than any exercise they may do while outdoors.

Taking a stroll can clear their minds like a form of meditation too, reducing their thinking activity and providing them with a form of freedom and escapism.

They also need regular outdoor break times at school to provide some relief from all that concentrating in the classroom.

Taking a walk or having a run around the yard helps them to go back into lessons with a clearer more focused mind, improving their productivity.

While ditching the pushchair and allowing toddlers to walk to the shops or school run with siblings is a great habitual form of exercise.

It may take a little longer to get where we're going, but rest assured, our children will eat and sleep better, and be in a better mood for it, making everyone's life happier. Nothing beats fresh air when it comes to getting a good night's sleep. Exposure to sunshine is also great for providing children with vitamin D, which is good for absorbing phosphate and calcium for healthy muscles, bones, and teeth. It's unlikely they'll get enough vitamin D from their diet, so sunshine is important. We'll go onto food in the final part of the U URSELF Routine, as well as Love, the most important ingredient. Love is what exercises our children's spirit and feeds their soul. But next, we'll look at sleep success. This can leave you free to enjoy some 'U Time' after they have worn themselves out playing!

CHAPTER 6:
SLEEP SUCCESS

TIME TO RELAX

A S WE KNOW, OUR children want to be with us all the time, flattering as this may be, we need our U Time, and they need their sleep. We have to find ways of encouraging them to want to go to bed and make bedtime a comfortable, relaxing experience they'll look forward to.

There's no Magical Cure, Sleeping Potions, or Sand Man in the world who is able to make our children sleep if they don't want to. Nobody can really **make** anybody sleep if they are not willing to do so, not even a Hypnotherapist like me. But there are ways in which we can help our children to relax and feel comfortable to sleep alone, soundly throughout the night.

Having quiet time to rest, relax, and daydream throughout the day is just as important as napping or sleeping at night.

Physical and mental capacity is impaired with too much activity and stimulation. This can be nearly as bad as none at all, making learning to relax a useful skill.

A day at School or Nursery sandwiched between child-minders, breakfast, or After School Clubs and family and friends is exhausting and demanding for our young children. This is just what we expect our children to do as part of their normal day.

Providing an adequate amount of activity for their age and allowing them plenty of time to do things, unrushed, can help them with all the comings and goings of everyday life.

For babies, any activity or visits should be short and sweet.

It's easy to overestimate what they need or what they are capable of tolerating. Routines such as nappy changing, bathing, or a trip to the shops are physically and mentally stimulating and exciting to them.

We might not feel we've exerted ourselves by taking a trip to the shops, followed by a visit to Auntie Sue's, but our baby will have.

Everything is new to them, and as they are constantly learning and encountering different experiences, we must allow plenty of periods for them to rest and process them.

Tempting as it is to play with them for hours on end with noisy, colourful toys, or wake them for a cuddle, passing them around cooing friends and family, this can all be too much for them to tolerate.

They soon become tired and irritable for what seems like no apparent reason. Then after such a busy day, we find ourselves puzzled as to why they cannot sleep, wondering why they are fighting it.

Why don't they just fall straight to sleep when we've tried our best all day to wear them out?

Well, the answer is, they simply cannot relax when they are irritable and past the point of sleep.

As they have no control over what happens to them, and no way to communicate their feelings, they become frustrated and upset.

And being picked up while fast asleep and moved can be a rude awakening that none of us would welcome.

Babies don't understand the journey has come to an end, and it's time to get out of the car, into the hustle and bustle of a busy supermarket. They were happy fast asleep. So, we have to be as sensitive, understanding, and accommodating to their needs as possible by offering uninterrupted, regular rest periods in order to prevent them becoming overtired and anxious.

RELIEVING ANXIETY

It's easy to spot if our children are overtired by how they behave.

Their emotions will be exaggerated, seeming unnecessary or inappropriate, displaying either frustration, sadness, anger, or all of those.

These emotions determine their behaviour, dictating how they act. Those feelings are there for a reason, they can help children regulate themselves if they understand and learn how to manage them.

When we recognise they're feeling emotionally tired, we can reassure them they are simply tired and will feel better after some rest. Most children become emotionally stable and behave appropriately with adequate rest.

After a good night's sleep or a short nap, they wake feeling refreshed and happy once again.

If not, then getting to the real problem and resolving the issues will be essential before expecting them to sleep well.

We need to make sure they are not anxious or stressed but are relaxed before bedtime.

Problems from the day can be left simmering in the back of their mind at bedtime, or fears over future events can bother them.

If they have things to face the next day which they are not looking forward to, such as a test at school or even a visit to the dentist, these worries can cause anxiety, manifesting as nighttime wakings.

We can help eliminate concerns they have by using Us Time to let them discuss issues openly with us each day and by offering them the chance to relax daily. Offloading some of their worries and relaxing more will provide time to think, reflect, and rationalise their thoughts and feelings (we will look at ways to do this in the next chapter when we look at Esteem and The Bother Box).

Sleep is vital in restoring children's mental and physical development and growth. As well as helping them to process the day's events, and to make sense of all they've learnt and experienced. Without adequate sleep, their mental and emotional capabilities are affected including their concentration and physical coordination. So, when tired, they are more accident prone and clumsy, their memory and learning abilities are affected, making it difficult to learn, remember, or concentrate, and their behaviour, moods, and emotions are all disrupted.

They can even experience disturbances that hinder the production of appetite controlling hormones which could be a contributing factor in possible weight gain.

PARENTS NEED SLEEP MORE THAN ANYTHING OR ANYONE ELSE

But what can be worse than a tired child?

A tired parent and child of course!

Lack of sleep is not only detrimental to children, it's also detrimental to our own mental state. If we can sleep soundly, undisturbed, and comfortable for around seven hours a night, we will be in a better position to deal with our children the next day.

But if we scrape by on a couple of broken hours here or there, we are likely to find ourselves overreacting on Auto Pilot Parenting Mode.

Everybody experiences times when they can't sleep at night, but if its ongoing with no apparent cause, and it isn't to do with physical factors such as temperature or something we can identify with such as pain, then we need to be proactive and find out what the cause is.

Being a parent is exhausting enough when we can sleep, let alone when we can't.

Our children can seem more challenging at those times when we are tired, and their unwanted behaviour can seem worse than it actually is.

Although their behaviour is actually worse when they don't get enough sleep. This is because the amygdala, the emotional part of the brain, is more active when a parent or child is sleep deprived. This explains why a tired child is usually very emotional for no reason and parents are angry, impatient, and frustrated more.

Together, a sleep deprived parent and child is an emotional disaster.

SLEEP DEPRIVATION

Lack of sleep can be detrimental to overall health and wellbeing, none of us should be deprived of the basic necessity to sleep.

Lack of sleep is also accumulative, so we have to catch up on sleep whenever we can.

Even if this means a nap in the day to make up for lost sleep at night. Parents sometimes avoid their children taking daytime naps, fearing they won't sleep as long at night, but the reverse is actually true.

Sleep deprived children have the worst sleeping habits, and those who nap in the day, actually sleep better at night. Children who need, but do not take a nap in the day, become overtired.

Once irritable, they find it difficult getting off to sleep or staying asleep throughout the night. This results in further irritability and oversensitivity the next day, causing challenging behaviour which can then lead to hyperactivity, especially at bedtime when they should be tired.

As children get older, days get longer, and nights shorter, then, more than ever, they need to rest from all the stimulation and digest the information and experiences from the day. We need to allow them the freedom to sleep whenever they feel the need to, not just when we want them or don't want them to. This way, they will sleep more soundly at night.

If their mind and body is telling them to sleep, no matter what their age, from five weeks to fifteen years, then they need it.

- How do you feel when you do not get your nightly quota of sleep?
- Do you ever feel so tired you struggle to get through the next day, only to go to bed that night unable to go to sleep?

Children do too! They get overtired and stimulated, resulting in unhealthy sleeping patterns. The only solution is for them to sleep whenever they can, to restore the balance and improve their sleeping habits.

- Think about a time when your child kept you awake all night for whatever reason. Then imagine how they must have felt and how tired they must have been the next day, probably ten times worse than you, I bet.

They do not understand why either we or they themselves are irritable, annoyed, upset, and emotional when tired. This becomes a sleep deprived combo not to be crossed.

TOO MUCH OR TOO LITTLE SLEEP?

Children have difficulty sleeping for all sorts of reasons, and it is possible that they can have too much sleep too. Routine is the only way to avoid too little or too much sleep. We need to know what time they go to bed, when they wake up, and how long they sleep for in total throughout the night and day and make changes where necessary. Once we can rule out the amount of time they are sleeping as the issue, the next avenue to explore is lack of recreation or exercise throughout the day, an issue the U URSELF Routine will have previously addressed.

Other reasons include: an inability to relax, their environment, nightmares, attention seeking, illness or pain, bedwetting, worrying, or more commonly their inability to personally pacify themselves to sleep alone.

All of these can be resolved once identified. Once they are, a nightly routine will emerge. But a routine won't guarantee our children will skip happily up the stairs to bed when the clock strikes seven. They'll still be reluctant to sleep and won't want to be isolated from the exciting activity of the home. Especially if they can hear us or their sibling's downstairs having fun, chatting or laughing at the TV, making bedtime an issue. One child may be younger, making their bedtime different from their older siblings, and this is where difficulties can lie.

Obviously, they won't want to be going to bed alone and will try any way they can to prevent this from happening, there's nothing we can do to make them sleep, however, we must still stick to their bedtime routine and make sure they go to their room at the appropriate time. Eventually, they will get used to this bedtime routine if it remains constant each evening, but there's little else we can do, it's their choice to sleep or not.

We know sleeping is an essential part of their daily routine, but they'll see it as a fun spoiler. Even when children are familiar with and understand the benefits of their routines, if absorbed in play or watching their favourite TV programme, they won't welcome the interruption those routines bring. Those things they enjoy doing will still always outweigh the benefits of going to bed to sleep. Unfortunately, that's life—they have to get used to it! But we can make it easier for them to accept. The best way to do that is to give them plenty of warnings and reminders, but the worst way is to suddenly end their fun. For example, if their bedtime is at seven, and as soon as the clock turns, we abruptly say to them:

'Come on, time for bed now!'

This can be an unwelcome surprise.

We need to gradually prepare our children with warnings and reminders first. Letting them know fifteen to ten minutes beforehand that it is nearly time for bed, gives them the chance to mentally and physically prepare themselves.

NO EXCUSE

Lack of sleep or poor-quality sleep will have a knock-on effect on every other part of the U URSELF Routine. Impacting upon everything they do, and every area of our children's lives. So, there can be no excuses to stay up just a bit later at bedtime. As mentioned earlier, it's normal for children to stall going to bed and suddenly get the urge to discuss events that happened in their day. Conveniently, these important matters can never wait, even though they've neglected to mention them for the previous six or more hours! In these situations, all we need to do to resolve such stalling is to let them know calmly that, in future, they will need to get ready for bed a little earlier, allowing them more time to chat about their day or brush their teeth. They may be a little more reluctant to chat about insignificant things when they realise it'll take up the last few minutes of their playtime in the evening. Alternatively (like previously suggested), you may find that your child is not dawdling deliberately to stay up later, but are taking their time because they are tired, and they may actually need to go to bed a bit earlier in future.

In these situations, all we need to do to resolve such stalling is to let them know calmly that in future, they will need to get ready for bed a little earlier, allowing them more time to chat about their day or brush their teeth.

They may be a little more reluctant to chat about insignificant things when they realise it'll take up the last few minutes of their playtime in the evening.

Alternatively, you may find that your child is not dawdling deliberately to stay up later, but are taking their time because they are tired, and they may actually need to go to bed a bit earlier in future?

First, we have to establish the real reasons keeping them awake. The excuses children give are not always what's preventing them from sleeping.

If they need the toilet five minutes after they've been, this is unlikely to be genuine. That's not to say our children are aware they are making excuses intentionally. Sometimes, they themselves don't know the real reason why they can't sleep, or why they've suddenly woken up halfway through the night.

We need to be aware though that whatever is keeping them from sleeping may not always be what they say.

CREATE THE RIGHT ENVIRONMENT

We can help make bedtimes more inviting and cosier for our children by creating the right environment. They need to feel comfortable, safe, and secure in their bed, knowing we are nearby if they need us. The things they tend to complain about, such as it's too cold, too light, too dark, or too scary won't always be the actual problem keeping them awake at night. These can be symptoms of their underlying anxiety about something they cannot relate or associate with, as being the real issue. Still, we need to address these first by creating the right environment, as they could be the cause of their sleep disturbances and need to be ruled out. Making sure they have a comfortable bed in their own room that is the right temperature (not too hot or too cold) with the right amount of bedding for the season is basic. Keeping noise down helps a light or sensitive sleeper too, and then if any of these things need altering, they are easy to do.

We can regulate temperature by opening a window, using a fan, putting the heating on, or providing extra blankets to create warmth.

Any signs of light will wake them easily and affect their body clock, so it's a good idea investing in blackout blinds or curtains. Avoiding the use of night lights or leaving landing lights on to comfort them is advisable, unless a one-off occasion such as to reassure them after a bad dream. If their physical environment is conducive to a good night's sleep, and hunger or overtiredness can be ruled out, yet they're still not sleeping through the night, something else is stopping them.

The usual culprits are illness, teething, and general pain.

ILLNESS, TEETHING OR GENERAL PAIN

If they have a fever or rash, are severely lethargic or unresponsive, then we can assume they're ill and need immediate medical attention. Teething or colic pain is not always visible but should subside of its own accord. Not helpful when trying to get a good night's sleep, I know, but there are over the counter remedies to help with this period. If constant over a few days, then it may not be teething. You should always contact your GP or out of hours if you are concerned. Even if it turns out to be teething, it's always best to get it checked, as our children can't let us know how they are feeling. But we can usually visually tell or sense if our children are responding differently, always follow your gut instinct, you know your child better than anyone else.

If unsure of the severity of their pain, there's a general test I like to recommend; next time they awake crying at night, let them hop into bed with you. If their pain magically disappears as soon as they jump into bed, it's not going to be pain keeping them awake.

We can be sure pain is not the cause of their sleeplessness because pain remains, regardless of where or who they sleep with.

If your child has a chronic medical condition or they have experienced stress or trauma, such as a parent leaving, you might feel sorry or guilty and encourage them to co-sleep with you for comfort. We need to reflect on the beliefs we have around our children's illnesses or circumstances to see if we are trying to overcompensate unnecessarily. Asking ourselves honestly whether they need our comfort to help them go to sleep, or whether we are interfering with their necessity to sleep alone because of our own emotions and beliefs.

Are we looking for comfort and company, or projecting our own fears and anxieties onto them?

If they are ill or under any sort of stress, they will need to sleep more than ever.

It's tempting to comfort and soothe them to sleep at these difficult times but when will the cut-off point be? The odd night is normal such as when they are sick or have had a bad dream, but if we make it a regular habit, we could still be sleeping with our teenagers!

I know all those attachment parents out there who believe co-sleeping is best will be going wild right now, everyone's entitled to parent their own way. I'm not saying my way is right and their way is wrong, but I have a strong attachment bond with my children, and we haven't co-slept.

Attachments come from love, and I believe routines provide all the love and comfort our children need to feel safe, secure, healthy, and happy. Routines make us proactive and responsive as parents, helping us meet the needs of our children before they desperately need them. Mums need a good night sleep to be emotionally and physically available to their children.

We also need to maintain a loving relationship with our partners to keep that bond strong too, something sharing a bed with our children makes impossible.

I've encountered many parents who have this attachment parenting style, who reject routine and let their children choose what they eat, wear, and when and where they sleep. Personally, I've not found these children any happier than any other child. I don't think children are experienced or capable of making the best choices for themselves. Given the choice, what child wants to go to bed early, on their own, or eat vegetables over chips?

That doesn't make us unfair for insisting they do though. But that's just my opinion. I'm an advocate for having close physical contact with your child. I kiss and cuddle my teenagers, and tell them I love them more than once every day, and have done so since they were born.

I also encourage them to be themselves and express how they feel and comfort and reassure them in times of need. But even though they are teenagers now, I still know what's best for them, and yes, they both still have a bedtime routine and are in bed by nine thirty on a school night. Call me old fashioned, but I want them to get all the rest they can and to feel refreshed for school the next day. Obviously, they'd prefer to be on their electronic devices, but we take them off them at bedtime so they can't. I'm not punishing them though. I'm helping them.

I encourage you to try letting your child lead the way if you want to experiment, then come back to a routine if that's not working.

It's a lot harder to provide consistent routines and to encourage our children to adopt healthy eating and sleeping habits, but that's the kind of nurturing that being a parent is all about. They can spend the rest of their adult lives making their own independent choices regarding what's right for them, until then, let's show them the healthiest ways.

As previously said, we offer our children routines for their own good, out of love. That doesn't mean that they are going to feel good about them in the beginning though.

If we have co-slept with our child for the last six years, but now would like them to move into their own bed in their own room, then we need to understand how they might feel. From their perspective, we're telling them to move from the shared, warm, safe comforts that they have always known to the cold, lonely, dark, unknown room across the landing.

Understandably, this new bedtime routine would upset them and seem more like a punishment for growing up. Their behaviour toward the changes, which could lead to angry or emotional protests or regressive behaviours such as, bed wetting or clinginess, is not intended to upset us for moving them into their own room. This is merely a normal reaction to change and to feeling afraid, anxious, or unsettled.

Regressive behaviours are their way of showing they still need us, or simply a coping mechanism to return to that time when they felt protected. In those moments, they need reassurance from us that everything will be okay. We must be understanding; soothing any fears they have in a calm and confident manner, whilst still communicating to them it's not a bad change in circumstances, it's just different.

ENURESIS BEDWETTING

Even if your child doesn't have an issue with bed wetting, I recommend you still read this section of the book, as the way we deal with this issue can be applied to any other we may encounter with improving our children's ability to help themselves.

The word enuresis derives from the Greek word 'to make water.'

When children initially start potty/toilet training, we can't expect them to be dry at night, overnight. Taking precautions to protect the bed such as using waterproof sheets and putting them in pullups to sleep in is a sensible option, along with expecting night-time wetting. While in a deep slumber, a child's muscles relax, making them unable to notice they need a wee until they are wet.

Regressive behaviours like bedwetting don't keep children awake though, sleeplessness is usually a symptom of laying in wet pyjamas or bedding. This can be a good motivator for not wetting the bed in the future, being wet, cold, and uncomfortable at night is not a nice feeling. As long as we don't get mad or upset with our child, this is how they will learn. We can help minimise the frustration to ourselves by changing sheets immediately, with minimum fuss, by always making their bed up twice, with two layers of waterproof sheets and normal sheets, just in case. This preparation means if they have an accident during the night, this limits the time and disruption of having to completely remake the bed. Simply throw off the top layer of wet sheets and waterproof, then underneath there will be more dry sheets and another waterproof sheet.

The actual issue of bedwetting does need exploring, but shouldn't prevent them from sleeping once their pyjamas and bedding has been changed.

If they are under five, then it shouldn't present much of a concern, especially in the toilet training stages. Making sure they use the toilet just before bed so they don't fall too deeply asleep and have an accident or wake up needing to go to the toilet in the middle of the night helps.

It's also a good idea to limit or stop the amount of fluid they drink prior to bedtime, offering only sips of water after four thirty pm, not milk or juice.

If they have not gone more than a few months dry at night after successful potty training in the day, they could have a developmental issue with their bladder, this can be hormonal and usually nothing to worry about. There are treatments available, and you can discuss these with your doctor. They could also have a small bladder capacity, if this is the case, you will probably notice that they urinate often throughout the day and find they are often desperate to go. They may wet at night due to emptying their bladder too frequently during the day. Either way, it's always advisable to consult your GP if you are concerned at all. If they're still bedwetting past six years of age, medical causes, as well as emotional factors, need to be looked into with their doctor to rule out any medical condition. Once they have been dry at night for several months to a year but then regress back to wetting at night, this nocturnal enuresis would suggest some sort of emotional stress or anxiety is responsible. If your GP has ruled out a physical problem such as a water infection, we can be proactive by looking for any apparent patterns, such as, do they only bed wet on certain days such as school days and not at the weekend?

Does it happen early on in the night or toward the end near morning time, when mum is on night watch or dad, how often a night/a week/ a month does it occur?

Are there any causes that influence the episode, such as, have they been emotional throughout the day because they fell out with their best friend or because dad is working away for the night?

Our children's fears and insecurities may seem so trivial and insignificant to us, but the smallest changes can have a huge impact. Looking at what is currently going on in other areas of their life is helpful. This is where the U URSELF Routine comes in handy, we can notice if another area such as their eating or exercising and play habits have changed too.

We may even already be aware of a possible cause of emotional stress for them such as having a new baby sibling, bereavement, moving to a new house, starting childcare, or a parent leaving home.

All of these things can be stressful for a small child, emotionally challenging, and are common underlying causes of regression. If stress and anxiety is the culprit, we have to handle the situation just as empathetically and positively as we would a physical medical condition that is also out of their control. This means praising them when they call out mid flow in the middle of the night for making good progress by noticing as it is happening, how we react in response will either help or hinder their progress at this point. Getting frustrated and saying things such as 'why didn't you get up and go straight to the toilet sooner, or, not again, or, I thought you had grown out of this' will only damage their self-esteem. This is the next part of the U URSELF Routine that we will explore in the next chapter 'Esteem'

What we want to do is focus on what we want them to achieve, not on what we don't want. Highlight the positives, such as the dry nights, and ignore the wet ones as best we can in the presence of our children. We can encourage and motivate them by offering to buy them some nice new PJs or perhaps bedding once they have successfully gone a whole week with a dry bed. How we phrase that reward is important, so keep it positive and focused on the dry bed. Instead of saying you can have a new pair of pjs if you don't wet the bed. We want to motivate them for staying dry, not put pressure on them not to wet the bed. When they do succeed going one night dry, we want to make the biggest fuss possible by showering them with praise and exaggerating how happy we feel for them, this is a chance to give their esteem a boost!

What we don't want our children to do is form a habit of bedwetting for either attention or feeling they have no control over their bedwetting. In no circumstances should we encourage this behaviour further and be tempted to bring back the pull up training pants for bed time. Once out of nappies and pull ups for several months, they are through with that baby phase of development. What they need most now is responsibility over their progress, they can't do this by going backward in how we treat them. They need to feel the wet cold discomfort to register they are wet, and this is something we want to motivate them to avoid in the future. A nice cosy, warm, dry, comfortable nappy or pullup, only motivates them to stay passive in their development. There's no urgency to progress by controlling their bladder. I've potty trained many toddlers over the years, and I've always used pants and knickers over commercial pull ups, a cheap pack of pants are usually cheaper than pull ups, and we can throw the soiled ones away if needs be, the same way we would a disposable nappy. But children learn far quicker by having accidents that they can feel and see. A pull up still feels like they are wearing a nappy, so I've found when parents choose this as a toilet training option, progress is much slower. I know pull ups are safer, easier, and less messy, but long term, they just delay the process. A couple of weeks of accidents, patience, and practise in real pants is the quickest and best long-term, effective, solution.

I always find that children who are given responsibility over their own lives, no matter how young, overcome challenges and progress quicker than those whose parents do everything for them and take control. This doesn't mean not helping or being involved as a parent and leaving them to sort out themselves, but taking a back seat at times. It's natural to want to love, protect, support, and do everything for them, but this can serve to make them feel as though they are a passenger on their journey of life; then events and experiences are out of their control and influence, and so there often seems little point in them making much of an effort to try or change. Helping strip their wet bedding off their bed and putting it in the washing machine with your help, then choosing what fresh bedding goes back on their bed next or what pyjamas to wear all involve them in their own self-care. Instead of feeling low self-esteem at what can be an embarrassing time, they now display self-love and respect. They are helping themselves, and we are allowing them to feel good in a situation that could make them feel bad if handled insensitively. It's their bedwetting issue to address and solve. This way, they'll look for solutions rather than feeling helpless and resigned to a life of wet nights, forming a habit that may be difficult to change later on. Now, in no instance are they responsible or to blame for their bedwetting, we are not suggesting that ever, but if anyone has any influence over changing it, **they** do!

And they will feel confident to try if they are given encouragement to do so. Our aim is for them to take conscious control over their issue, not be a passive allower. Fostering this self-reliance is what will help them to build self- confidence, making them feel they can handle situations themselves. They don't feel guilty or as though we are punishing them if they feel they are helping in some way and having choices and responsibility. Children want to be independent, that is why there is often conflict and tantrums, because they want to be able to do things for themselves. Managing conflict and tantrums is covered extensively in my other book, *The Powerful Proactive Parent's Guide to Present Parenting*. But let's just say for now that their bad behaviour isn't always that bad. The less of a big issue we can make out of their bed wetting, and the bigger the fuss we can make over a dry bed, the quicker the preferred behaviour will become a habit. We can best help, however, by uncovering the source of their underlying emotional issue or anxiety they are currently experiencing and focusing on that, rather than the presenting symptom of bedwetting. Once that has been addressed, the bed wetting, in time, if not left long enough unaddressed to become a habit, will resolve itself.

Their anxiety and fears may also manifest in other ways such as nightmares.

NIGHTMARES

They could be seeking comfort and reassurance because of fear of the dark. Anxiety causes sleeplessness. However, they won't know or understand why they are having difficulty sleeping.

When a child is faced with an angry, tired, version of a parent, demanding:

'Why are you awake at this time?'

Then saying, 'I had a nightmare' may be the only logical defence they can find, and one most parents sympathise with.

If they said 'I don't know,' they'd be scolded back into bed.

At some point, all children experience anxiety or fear at night time, either before going to sleep or during the middle of the night.

Occasionally, it's perfectly normal and can be due to:

- A bad dream or an irrational fear of something they've watched on TV or heard about in the news.
- Difficulties at school with teachers or their work
- Bereavement/change of circumstances in the family.
- Fear of themselves, their habits and behaviours, especially if they don't understand their own feelings such as anger or sadness.
- Experiencing difficulties in relationships with friends or fitting in with different groups of people.
- Feeling overwhelmed with all their newfound responsibilities and the separateness from us that growing up brings.

It's in the quiet loneliness of night that all of these worries about their past, present, and future become apparent and magnified.

As they struggle to make sense of life and the world they inhabit whilst laying in their bed awake with a headful of active thoughts, or while fast asleep, jumbled up in dreaming, these fears and anxieties surface. Nightmares present a way to digest those thoughts and feelings safely or to bring those worries and anxieties into the open. Shadows dancing on the ceiling, mysterious noises outside their bedroom window, or waking up in different surroundings to where they fell asleep causes children's imagination to soar. Understanding their anxieties is key to curing and resolving bedtime, as well as daytime issues. Nightmares can feel really real to children and extremely frightening. Instead of dismissing their fears with 'Stop being so silly, it's only a dream, be a big boy/girl and go back to sleep'. Which does nothing to make them feel safe or to ease them back to sleep, listen to them sympathetically instead. Then, chatting and distracting them by getting them to think something nice instead, like an upcoming party or holiday, changes their focus from dwelling on the bad dream to thinking of something more pleasurable, changing how they think and feel. Reassuring them everybody has these dreams sometimes, letting them know we are close by, and leaving the bedroom doors ajar or light on in the landing also helps, but don't make lights on a habit. Also, buying or making a dream catcher to go over their bed, explaining it catches all the bad dreams, or telling them the Sleep Fairies and Elves are watching over them, keeping them safe and protecting them as they sleep, reassures.

Nightmares are common and no real cause for concern, sometimes they can be due to eating or drinking certain types of food and drink before bed time, over tiredness, or in some cases, they happen prior to feeling unwell or getting an infection or temperature. But If they experience frequent, prolonged nightmares, there's likely something worrying them that needs addressing. Nightmares will persist until issues are dealt with. Children may act carefree throughout the day, but night time offers time for those concerns they are concealing to express themselves freely. Those bad dreams and fears of Monsters or Ghosts are symbolic and represent emotions.

Our wrath on top of their original fear makes them feel frightened, all alone in the dark. Scared and paralysed by fear but afraid to turn to us in their distress through fear of being shouted at for waking us up, adds to their anxiety. Uncovering and dealing with their fears or anxiety should help to restore a sound night's sleep.

ATTENTION SEEKING

Some children experience separation anxiety and wake in the middle of the night for reassurance. Usually, all they need is to know we are close by and a reassuring kiss and a cuddle will help them drop off to sleep.

Other times, they could be seeking attention. We have to learn how to discern between genuine night time fears and playing a game to stay awake.

We can't always rely on what our children say, but how they look and act will give us a clue. Taking into account what they say, how they say it, and their general body language. They can't act true pain or fear, something will give them away. Likewise, if they say it's just a bad dream but we sense real fear or anxiety, we should delve a little deeper.

If, however, they say they are scared but are concealing a grin, we will know the difference. Taking everything into consideration, including what's currently going on in our children's lives, looking at past unresolved issues that could be affecting them and causing genuine nightmares or fears is the best, proactive approach. Is there any traumatic experience or some sort of separation or upheaval that has happened in their life that could be resurfacing?

Reasons may not be obvious at first. It could even be something we have overlooked at the time as insignificant. Children can be sensitive souls and are vulnerable to misinterpreting things.

Being unaware of how things can affect them means it may be necessary to dig a little deeper until something comes up. Children will be as puzzled by their fears or nightmares as we are. They are often unable to relate them to past experiences or future concerns, leaving us to make that connection if we can.

THE ABILITY TO PERSONALLY PACIFY

If your child has never been able to sleep independently throughout the night on a regular basis, and there's nothing new or significant going on in their lives, then it's likely they've not had the chance to learn how to personally pacify themselves.

Everybody wakes up to use the toilet, have a drink, or change sleeping positions throughout the night, so there's no need to worry when our children wake up, this is perfectly normal and necessary.

The problem is our children's inability to get back off to sleep.

If they don't know how to settle themselves alone back off to sleep, or we are in the habit of helping them, they'll rely on us to do so.

Unfortunately, the more we try to help them, the less likely they will be to learn how to develop the ability to personally pacify themselves back to sleep, expecting us to help them every time they wake up, which could be several times throughout the night. They can at times wake up startled and confused, crying out, but If we keep going into their room, offering them a bottle, breast, dummy, teddy, blanket, cuddle, rock, stroke, or lullaby, then they won't learn to naturally fall back off to sleep. And we'll still be singing lullabies and stroking our teenagers until they find us embarrassing and tell us to stop.

Can you imagine the next ten years without a good night's sleep?

If you don't relish that thought, then try creating the habit of them dropping off to sleep unaided by playing audio meditations as they go to sleep. This won't work when they suddenly wake in the middle of the night, but they need to have their own pacifiers in place for those times.

COMFORTERS

Anything that pacifies, soothes, and comforts a child has a place in their life.

Comforters, such as dummies, teddies, or blankets provide a sense of security and company for children, but if they can't find them in the middle of the night, they will wake us to.

As long as we resist our urge to go in and rescue the dummy, they'll get better at finding it and personally pacifying themselves back off to sleep, helping everyone sleep better.

Children are more content and find it easier to fall asleep and are easier to reassure in times of distress when they have a comforter. Until, of course, those comforters are taken away, lost, or we've forgotten them.

Then the absence of their teddy, dummy, or chewed familiar old blanket mean hours of tears and tantrums and no sleep. Children come to rely on and forge strong attachments with comforters because they provide comfort, companionship, familiarity, and love.

They offer the familiar feel and smell or rhythmic sucking they have learnt to help soothe and relax them. Pacifier's themselves are not the problem. Children who lack comforters only end up sucking their thumbs or something else as a substitute anyway, such as clothing labels.

It's the association children make when falling asleep that cause issues, such as having a bottle or a stroke.

Then, when these are absent, they find going to sleep difficult. Relying on us to provide comfort such as a breast to suckle them to sleep. Then, without us, getting back off to sleep alone in the middle of the night when they awake as a natural part of their sleep cycle is difficult.

SLEEPING SUCCESS

Babies sleep undisturbed and better alone. As long as we have a loving bond, this will give them the security to sleep. Children who are used to sleeping with their parents or using them as comforters, feel insecure when that parent is unavailable. Fostering independence from an early age, coupled with lots of love and Us Time throughout the day, creates confident, secure, self-reliant individuals.

When children associate going to sleep alone in the dark in their own room, this is what they will expect as normal. This will be enough to comfort and soothe them naturally to sleep, unaided. Starting out this way early on with a sleep routine at the same time each evening assures the best sleeping success.

We are not being cold or unloving. They need their sleep, and we need ours too to be the best we can be. If you find your baby cries or is fractious when you put them to bed initially, try walking around their bedroom with the light off, pretending to do other things such as folding clothes. They will feel comforted by your presence, but you need to leave the room as soon as they settle.

REGULAR ROUTINES

Having a regular time to go to bed each and every evening is key. We won't be able to make them sleep while in bed, but our job is done when we make sure they are tucked up at a set time. There's no need to argue with them to sleep, at this stage, we are just establishing a routine. They will fall asleep of their own accord when their bed becomes their cue to, and there's nothing else stimulating on offer. Setting a regular bedtime and sticking to it helps develop certain sleep wave patterns. These don't change at the weekend; their body clock will send them to sleep and wake them up the same time on a Saturday, as it would on a Monday. So, bedtime needs to be consistent even at weekends. We can't actually force our children to sleep. We just need to provide bedtime routines for them to follow as best they can. Bath, massage, brush teeth, bedtime story, lights out.

Then we can feel confident our part as loving, responsible, Proactive Parents is done. Regular routines in all areas such as eating and exercise are imperative in helping children to sleep well, that's why embracing all parts of the U URSELF routine is essential to our children's well-being and feeling good, which we will explore further now in the following chapter—Esteem.

CHAPTER 7:
ESTEEM—TEACHING OUR
CHILDREN TO BE SELF-ISH

CHILDREN NEED TO BE SELF-ISH
Selfish

THROUGHOUT THIS BOOK, WE are preparing our children physically, emotionally, and socially for life in the real world without us. This doesn't just mean when they grow up and leave home, it means when they have to go anywhere or do anything without us, such as starting school and childcare. The foundations we build to support them now, such as having routines and fostering self-confidence and self-belief within them will be essential. By the end of this book, we will undoubtedly feel more confident as parents, and hopefully, that will reflect in how we make our children feel too.

Our children are our prize possession, so we have to make them feel like the prize. Their self-esteem will be determined by the respect, admiration, and appreciation they receive.

That's why we are ultimately aiming for a Selfish child!

This word is not to be misunderstood or taken in a negative, egocentric context though. Here, when referring to making our children more selfish, we mean we are helping them to build more of the five self's below:

SELF-BELIEF: What our children believe they can do, achieve, or be.

SELF IMAGE: How our children view themselves, for example; how they see their intelligence or physical attractiveness.

SELF RESPECT: How well our children look after and treat themselves generally, including diet and exercise.

SELF CONFIDENCE: How our children act or assert themselves and how sure they are in their own ability.

SELF ESTEEM: How our children regard and acknowledge their good qualities and think and feel about themselves in general. Including how much they like themselves or believe that they are a good person, deserving of all the good that life has to offer or not. And how close their 'real self' is in alignment with their 'ideal self'. That is—how they feel they measure up against the version of themselves they think they should or the way they want to be.

These five selves all impact upon one another, but not always. One child may have a good self-image and find themselves attractive, but may not have any confidence in their academic ability. Another may excel at sports but have low self-esteem in every other area of their life, it just depends on what they place value or importance on in their lives.

Children just want to fit in and feel like everyone else. If such a definition as 'normal' exists, then that's how we want to help our children feel.

We can do this by validating at every opportunity that how our children feel is normal and okay, such as, it's normal to get angry when someone snatches a toy off them. This can be difficult, as our first response to our children's undesirable behaviour is to insist they act or feel a certain way that's more acceptable. For example, if they get angry and shout or hit out at the injustice they think they've received from the other child who snatched a toy off them, our first reaction would be to tell them not to be angry and that 'two wrongs don't make a right' and usually we insist they say sorry to the other child they have upset, but we can often forget to validate that their feelings of anger were normal under those circumstances. Because they can't articulate in words to the child who snatched the toy off them how they feel, they get frustrated and angry. Yet most if not all children would feel the same. The reason we don't validate their anger is because we don't like to see our children angry as it can be an unkind, ugly emotion at times, so we try to prevent or stop it, and this serves to make our children feel bad or wrong for feeling angry.

We can only go so far in helping our children though, they play the most important part themselves, so it's time to step back and allow them to be themselves. This should come naturally, yet with so much influence and input from others, over time, they can find being themselves is not so good. That's when they try to change themselves to fit in or to become accepted by others. This can be damaging to their self-esteem and can affect their self-confidence in all areas of their lives, sometimes creating unhealthy habits.

KNOW THYSELF

Our children knowing themselves is essential to their happiness, health, and success. But only they can learn who they really are and discover what they really like, without knowing this, they will be aiming at the wrong goals in life. Socrates the philosopher once said 'Know thyself' but this can be perplexingly difficult for our children at times as they are constantly changing. We can support them in their uncertainty by helping them form a positive impression of themselves and life in general while they are young. This is important because they carry their beliefs about themselves as a child into adulthood, and those beliefs determine what they do and who they become in the future. Our children will become whoever they believe themselves to be. Yet a large contribution of beliefs and their self-image will be formed from other people's perspectives. Unfortunately, other people's negative opinions about them can stick in their young, impressionable minds, even as adults. These create self- limiting beliefs' that can hold them back if not challenged.

SELF-LIMITING BELIEFS

If not overcome, these self-limiting beliefs can become the enemy to success and happiness. Especially potent are those beliefs created by authority figures such as from parents and teachers. If a child is told that they 'Will never be any good at_____' fill in the blank with a subject, these negative comments stick in their subconscious mind. They then believe them to be true, even if years later they have proved them to be wrong. Often, they will look for ways to prove those authority figures right, albeit subconsciously. We call this confirmation bias. Then, when their negative self-beliefs and attitude inevitably causes them to fail, they'll think 'Well, the teacher did say I would never be any good at it, and look—they were right!'

We need to challenge our children's self-limiting beliefs and find out where they came from and whether or not the source was correct or reliable? Seeking to prove them wrong, rather than right, and reinforcing the things that our children are good at and can do. There will always be things they find challenging, but they shouldn't avoid them or believe they are unachievable, nothing is impossible with the right support and encouragement.

OUT OF DATE INFO

Children under seven are very impressionable, they particularly take in things that upset them or stand out as most significant, especially traumatic events. They then sort and store these experiences in their subconscious mind for future reference, which then becomes available to assist them in the future. This is helpful if the information is right or is intended to keep them safe in some way, but sometimes it can be wrong, misguided, and outdated. Information received while young is based on a young child's perspective and may not be appropriate to them as they get older. Even when they have grown up and outgrown it, they may still be acting, thinking, or feeling based on those past experiences.

Self-limiting beliefs stack up, and children are constantly adding to them over the course of their lives as they discover more and more things they can't do.

This causes them to create fears and restrictions on themselves, and if others impose limiting expectations upon them, they add to a child's own self-limiting beliefs, especially if they believe them or they remember situations or comments that reinforce them. Fortunately, with the right encouragement, support, and belief, children can combat and overcome these self-limiting beliefs.

Children believe others over themselves most of the time, so, if they have fallen off a bike many times, their mind will tell them 'You can't ride a bike.'

But if we can convince them that they can. With some patience, persistence, and practice, they'll believe us and start practicing until they eventually learn how to ride that bike. Because we have said and believe they can, they start to believe it themselves. As Proactive Parents, we need to show them that their limiting beliefs are inaccurate and find evidence to support why they can do something that they believe they can't.

If they say they are no good at sport, we can remind them of an occasion when they were, such as when they came first in the egg and spoon race. Our job is to question their beliefs and point out how vague they are being, by asking them in a confused tone:

'Sport? ... What sport in particular are you no good at?

And:

'What do you mean by no good exactly?' This will make them think less generally.

If they reply; 'I mean I'm no good at rugby.'

We could say; 'Well that's not all sport, that's just one activity, but why do you think you are no good at rugby anyway?'

They might reply with; 'I didn't score a try last week.'

We could then ask; 'Did everyone else score one?'

They may respond; 'No only two people scored a try.'

We could continue; 'So are none of the others any good at rugby also?'

To which they would have to honestly reply; 'No some are good.'

STICKY LABELS

Regardless of talent, ability, qualifications, experience, money, or even if they follow 'The Seven Steps to Success' which we will reveal later on in chapter 11, none will make a difference without our children having Self-belief. If they don't believe that they can do something, then they won't be able to do it, even if we are really encouraging and believe in them. Their self-belief influences everything, including their performance throughout school and academic potential.

These self-beliefs often lead to success in areas they feel confident and believe they can do well in, but in those they don't, they'll likely avoid or not do so well in.

There will be a variety of subjects in school, some they will not always enjoy, but they will be more likely to persist if they believe they can achieve good results in them, and we can help them build their self-belief by:

- Believing in their capabilities:—If we do, then they will.
- Giving them responsibilities—Showing them that we believe and trust in them when it comes to important matters and giving them responsibilities makes them more responsible.
- Helping them—If they are struggling in any subject at school, or any other area of their lives for that matter, mentally, physically, spiritually, or emotionally, we can help them overcome these obstacles and succeed by getting them the help, support, and resources they lack or need.
- Encouraging them to be proactive—Taking action will give them the confidence to believe that they can achieve anything, even if they fail. It's the fear of not being able to do a thing that stops them from believing they can. They have to gain confidence through achievement, and self-belief through doing and proving to themselves they can.
- Complimenting them—Pointing out their efforts as much as their achievements and being specific. A general 'Well done' is not enough, we need to elaborate. Well done for what exactly?

To replicate their success, they need to know exactly what it was they did so well in order for them to apply that to something else in the future.

- Not over doing it—If we are too general or praise them when it's not due, then they will not believe our praise to be genuine. Our children's self-belief comes from the support and encouragement of others, including ourselves, but words of encouragement or trying to boost their ego with praise alone, will not work. They have to believe and feel good about themselves for genuine reasons. No matter how many times we tell them they are the best at something if they know they aren't, they won't be fooled. And the more they perceive us to be lying about what they think they can do, the less likely they will be to accept our genuine praise or compliments.

No matter how much praise we give or belief we have in our children, it's what they believe and achieve, and whether it's important to them or not, that counts, which is down to their own self-image.

Self Image

If they are not happy with their self-image, this can affect their self-esteem and confidence in all areas of their life. What they believe to be true about themselves can influence the people around them, including friends and partners and how well they interact with others.

Also, how they learn, their goals and aspirations in life, including grades at school, choice of career, and the habits they adopt. As already said, it's the picture they hold of themselves about the type of person they are that will ultimately determine the individual they become when they are older and can influence how happy, healthy, and successful they are. However, it's not always a true reflection of their character, but is usually based on the information received from others such as teachers, family, and friends.

FITTING IN

Children will be influenced and compare themselves against others, such as celebrities and friends. At times, they may not like their self-image and want to be like someone else. This can affect their behaviour and the way they look and dress, manifesting into whatever fad or fashion is popular with others to fit in and be accepted. We don't need to try and change them, no matter how extreme or unflattering their look is; any reaction could be just the attention they are seeking. If they want to stand out and be different from their parents, our disapproval may be just what they are looking for. These normal phases come and go, next week, it may be something different and possibly less appealing, so all we can do is ride it out with as little resistance as possible. From clothes, hairstyles, piercings, to body art, it's their way of demonstrating their selfish-ness. Hopefully, it's just a phase or fashion statement, but if we fight against it, we help to keep it in fashion for longer. Sometimes, their need to be different may mean they choose a look that's not even popular with peers, this demonstrates their confidence to stand out and be who they are. If we judge or criticize them for being themselves, this can do more damage than wearing some unusual clothes or dying their hair. They will only develop problems with their self-image if others do. If we can accept and approve of them for who they are, they will also be able to approve and accept others, as well as themselves, for who they are. All children are and should be unique, we need to let them know that it's no good being a sheep who just follows the herd, and it's okay, even admirable, to have their own style and personality. This way, they know they don't have to be perfect, but they can be perfectly themselves and they realise how special they are to us for who they are. We don't have to change them; we just need to reinforce their positive attributes. But we shouldn't wait until they hit those dreaded rebellious teens, by then it will be too late to help them. At this age, no input we offer will be seen as helpful. It's how we help and prepare them now while they are young that will build love and trust in us in the future. We can help them create a positive self-image now by;

- Making them feel loved and accepted—Embracing their unique style, even if we don't like it.
- Highlighting their positive attributes—By reinforcing their good attributes, we take all the focus off what they don't like about themselves, helping them to see what's good instead, offering a better overall balanced view.
- Listening and talking to them and understanding how they feel and view themselves—It's normal to find something they dislike about their body, and if this is the case, we should listen and talk to them about it. They may have an exaggerated view of something or even an unjustified one.
- Helping them to understand that beauty is in the eye of the beholder—We don't all like tall, dark, and handsome, and what's handsome to one, may not be to another. We all have different features we look for in others.
- Not comparing them to others—If they compare themselves to others, we need to explain that no one's perfect, and that celebrities in magazines are airbrushed and made up by a team of experts. By showing them unflattering pictures of celebs on the internet, they can see how everyone can have an off day. Our children need to realise they can be just as good looking as anyone else with the right tools, techniques, and people to help them.
- Appreciating themselves and what they do have—instead of comparing what they don't have—Getting our children to appreciate what they have naturally is vital to their self-image. They may have naturally blonde or curly hair that others pay to achieve through chemicals. By them understanding that no one is ever one hundred percent satisfied with how they look all the time and others want what they have too, can encourage them to like themselves for who they are instead of comparing their beauty to false or unrealistic images and expectations. A tall person for instance won't make a very good jockey but they would make a great model. It's about getting them to appreciate and work with what they have got going for them naturally already, and using it.

- Giving them opportunities to release their vulnerabilities—Feeling comfortable in their own skin increases the more often they show themselves in front of other's. If they go swimming or to Gymnastic classes for example, over time, the less self-conscious they will feel, as they will notice everyone else's different shapes and sizes too, and instead of feeling vulnerable or exposed, they will get familiar and accepting of how they look, feeling less embarrassed.
- Observing and educating—If we notice them looking at their own image in the mirror more often or becoming obsessed about what they wear, weigh, or eat, we need to discuss this with them. Explaining how eating less doesn't make them lose weight, but how eating more of the right type of nutritious food will. Stressing how looking good is about feeling good and respecting the body they were born with.

Self Respect

Once they have a positive self-image, they will develop self-respect and will want to do all they can to take good care of themselves, such as; eating healthily, making time to play and relax in equal balance, taking regular exercise, brushing their hair and teeth, sleeping enough, keeping their personal space such as bedrooms reasonably clean and tidy, respecting their belongings such as hanging up their school uniforms as well as taking care of toys and computers. We can offer them the opportunity to develop and maintain their self-respect by teaching them how to do these things for themselves through their routines. Also, by making them accountable for their own health and safety, especially if they have allergies or need medication, such as an Asthma Pump or Epi Pen.

Self Love

Self-respect leads to self-love. We prove we love our children through the U URSELF Routine, and this makes them more inclined to value and look after themselves. As they get older, this can be a deterrent from risky behaviour, as they are more likely to keep themselves safe and healthy if they are already in the habit of doing so from a young age. They will also worry about hurting us because when they feel loved, loving, and lovable, they will understand how much their behaviour will impact us, as much as themselves. This may prevent them experimenting in the future with something that could damage their health or effect their safety such as; smoking, drinking alcohol, taking drugs, or having unprotected sex. Chances are, they will not feel the need to engage in these kinds of activities so much if they value their own health and safety. This won't be easy for them, as everyone wants to be in the 'Cool Gang' who experiment with risky pastimes and behaviours. Being Self-ish and standing out proud as an individual, is what we need to instil in our children. It takes a lot of self-respect and confidence to say 'No' when others are classed as being cool for saying 'Yes'.

Self Confidence

As we have seen from chapter one, confidence is key to setting you free, and it's the same for our children. When they feel confident in themselves and their abilities, they have freedom. Freedom from doubt, fear, anxiety—freedom to take a chance and fail. However, children are constantly confronted with firsts, and it can be hard for them to feel confident meeting new people or in new situations, even if they have the ability or good social skills. But if they don't have these things and feel inadequate, then feeling confident can be a real challenge. Capabilities and qualifications are useless if they lack the confidence to use them effectively. Unfortunately, if they give up, believing they can't do something, they lower their self-confidence further.

Lack of confidence is just a fear of the unknown or failure. Once they overcome this and take action, they can increase their confidence even if they fail. We can also restore their confidence by reminding them of their past achievements using their; School Reports, photos, certificates, journals etc., and by encouraging them to learn something new that we know they can accomplish, but that still offers a challenge. Confidence breeds confidence, but it's not an innate attribute, our children need to acquire it. They were very confident as a baby, otherwise how else would they have ever taken their first steps and learnt how to walk?

They would have fallen down and failed many times but still would have got back up and eventually learnt how to walk. At that time though, they would have been surrounded by a Cheering Squad of Raving Fans, encouraging them every step of the way. But as they grow up, that cheering squad turns into the Critic's Brigade, with parents, peers, teachers, family, and friends all telling them what they have done wrong, how they could improve, and what they can't or shouldn't do. These enforce their limitations, but by championing what they can do, and positively reframing situations, we free their self-doubt and limitations and coach them instead of criticise.

REFRAME THE SITUATION

Our children will be confronted with unfavourable situations, but we can avoid that affecting their confidence if we reframe the situation for them, changing any negatives into positives. When bad things happen, at first the positives may not be apparent, but there is usually something good to come out of everything, good or bad, if we look hard enough to find it.

Should they come home from school upset because they did not get the leading role in the school concert, we can help them to change how they feel and view the rejection by saying;

'It's a shame you didn't get the role you wanted, but your Teacher obviously could see your talent was better put to use singing in the choir instead.'

By distracting from what's upsetting them and focusing on the positive reasons why their teacher did not choose them, we acknowledge how they are feeling and at the same time, help them to feel better about the situation, as well as themselves. We are not offering sympathy and adding to the woe is me for not being picked as leading role, and we are not implying tough luck, that's life, deal with it, either. Neither are we lying and giving them a false belief of their abilities just to boost their ego by saying that we don't understand why they didn't get the leading role, as they are the better actor. It's good to boost their confidence, but it's never a good idea to blatantly tell them they are better at something than someone else is, or good at something when they are not. This can end up being more damaging to their confidence and self-esteem when they realise that actually they aren't. We have to be truthful in such a way that our children still feel good about themselves regardless. When being honest over something that we know will upset them, it's best to sandwich it between two positives that are true to deflect the negative, i.e.;

'Well done for making it onto the school magazine. It's a shame you weren't chosen as a journalist like you wanted, but as a photographer capturing the images, you will be involved in all the action. And as they say, one picture can say more than a thousand words ever could!'

Here in the above example, we've acknowledged their achievement to be chosen to work on the school magazine, this way their confidence stays intact, but we also understand they didn't get the position they originally wanted. Yet we reassure them that as photographer, they have a just as good, if not even better, position.

SHOW OFF

We want them to feel good about themselves and to showcase their talents whenever possible. Letting them shine and show off their talents is important to their self-confidence. A self-confident child should be admired and encouraged. It's not going to make them big headed by acknowledging what they do well. We won't build their confidence by pointing out their failures or shortcomings or by lecturing them on what they don't already know or in proving them wrong. Sometimes, the cleverest way to act as a parent is dumb, being underestimated by our children keeps them on their toes and us ahead. When they impart their knowledge upon us, instead of feeling patronized or getting upset and declaring we've forgotten more than they will ever know, we can just smile and listen interestedly at what they have learnt. All that matters is that we know we are right and that our children are happy. Then our annoyance will change to pride as we realize how clever they are becoming. Eventually, we'll start to feel flattered that all they really want to do is show us how smart they are and impress us.

CRITISISM THE CONFIDENCE CRUSHER

Criticism is a Confidence Crusher. We can choose to crush criticism and instead of saying, 'You did that wrong, you should have done it like this,' we could try changing criticism into positive statements like; 'That's interesting, I never thought of doing it that way. I wonder if there are any other ways you can find of doing it?' This way, we not only build our children's confidence, but they take our advice as helpful and supportive. Usually, they already know their failings and wont welcome being reminded of them. If they didn't do well in their spelling test at school, they will be aware of it, so our energy and time would be better spent offering reassurance, guidance, and support. Helping them to practise next week's spellings, and keeping a positive attitude for next time, will get them to forget their past mistakes that they can't change and focus on their future success that they do have control over. It takes a while for our children to believe anything counterproductive, and luckily, they instantly thrive on good feedback they are given. That's why praising their efforts not only their achievements and reminding them of their strengths will help them achieve more than giving constructive criticism.

AFFIRMATIONS

Where negative statements can be accepted as true in our children's mind, so too can positive statements. We call these Affirmations, and they can be used to counteract and overcome a negative, unhelpful belief, or reaffirm something wanted, bringing about positive thoughts and feelings. They're positive statements said as if they are already true. Try this little exercise now.

Say three times with a big smile on your face;

'I feel good.'

'I feel good.'

'I feel good.'

And feel how good that feels. You can literally feel how good that feels, can you not?

While saying it, we simply can't, but not feel good. We may feel a bit silly saying them at first, but children are less self-conscious. They will find affirmations a fun way to program their minds and to plant and grow positive suggestions in their subconscious. But what's really great is if they can accept these positive suggestions while young, then there will be less reprogramming to be done as they get older. To encourage this habit, they need to think of a positive statement in the present tense that they can relate to. The language needs to be simple, using words they would use in everyday speech and that's appropriate for their understanding. If too complex, they'll be less likely to understand or take the statements on board. It's better they choose their own affirmations they feel comfortable with saying, these can be written if the child is old enough to compliment and reinforce the verbal affirmation but are best said aloud repeatedly. They need to be short, simple, positive, uplifting, motivating, and believable. Such as; 'I am now learning more and more every day.' Repetition is key to affirmations and the more they practise using positive affirmations, the easier they get and the better they start to feel about themselves and their capabilities.

This probably won't surprise you to know, but while children are speaking and thinking positively about themselves, it's impossible for them to think negatively, and then fear, worry, anxiety, anger, and frustration disappear. This is useful if they are struggling in some area, such as learning how to read, instead of listening to their self-defeating mental chatter, they can replace it with positive self-talk and could say;

'I enjoy learning how to read, reading is fun, and I am now finding it easier and easier to read.' We can clearly understand how this approach is more helpful than what children usually say such as;

'I can't read, I hate reading, it's hard.' Convincing themselves with their own words that they cannot read, not realising that they are the ones holding themselves back. Children confuse lack of experience and confidence in something, such as reading, as a lack of ability, and believe they do not, cannot, and will never be able to do it. Any mistakes they encounter only reinforce this, knocking their confidence further, we can minimise the risk of this happening by introducing our children to the 'As If' game.

PLAYING THE AS IF GAME

Playing the 'As if Game' can help get over these initial self-doubts. It's a fun make believe game, that children naturally play when role playing. They can use this to purposefully daydream and use their creative imaginations when they want to achieve something to enhance their chances of success. If they can use their vivid imaginations to visualise what they want to be, have, or achieve, they will be halfway there to achieving it. This method focuses their attention on what they want, instead of what they don't want. Getting them to visualise attaining their goals prepares them for what's to come and is a safe way for them to practice trying out new things beforehand. This makes them more inclined to have a go in reality, and as long as they imagine a positive outcome, this can increase their confidence and motivation. Whatever their mind can conceive and believe, they will be able to achieve, so if they can imagine themselves winning the race at sports day and see it in their mind as a mental picture, chances are, they could win the race on the actual day at school. All athletes use these visualisation techniques before they compete, and they do work because our minds can't differentiate between a real or an imagined event. That's why when our children worry, they experience real physical anxiety, and when they imagine winning, they feel happy.

This 'As If' game doesn't guarantee they will win the actual race on the day though, but the chances are, they will do a lot better if they play this game, than if they don't. They will always increase their chances of success when they use their creative imagination to see the end result of what they want, the way they want it to be, and as if it has already happened. But it's not a magic formula or guarantee, practice produces results. When young, they can role play this in a game of make believe and draw the story with their happy ending. Then when old enough, they can relax with their eyes closed prior to sleep, or when they awake, as this is when their mind will be more receptive to positive suggestions, and visualize hearing, feeling, seeing, or even smelling any situation that they need confidence in. If they have to perform in a school assembly, they can; imagine walking onto the stage and seeing all the parents' faces smiling at them, see or hear themselves delivering their lines clearly and confidently, and feel how good it feels when the audience claps at the end of the performance. The more they can practice in their mind how they would like an unfamiliar circumstance to be, the more relaxed, prepared, and confident they will feel when they have to face the situation in reality.

Self Esteem

The more confident our children become, the better they will feel. The level of our children's self-esteem is the culmination of self-belief, self-image, self- respect, and self-confidence. And positively combined, all of these together determine their overall happiness. We won't always understand how they feel or know what they are thinking, but we can help them to understand their own thoughts and feelings better. Encouraging them to keep a journal of daily events in their life, recording their emotions as much as achievements, helps them to see the part they play in their life and how other people or situations can make them feel. Noting all the positive comments received, such as praise about their homework from a teacher or a compliment from a friend, can help to pick them up whenever they are experiencing a low day and deflect away from any negative comments. Our children are only limited by their thoughts, and these can be changed. Whatever we believe is a barrier to their health, happiness, or success, we need to remove, overcome, or get around it before they believe it. There are so many opportunities and resources available today, our children are more fortunate than any other generation before them, so nothing should hold them back. Believe that they can do anything, and they will too!

When we are proactive in our approach to parenting, we endeavour to meet our children's needs, before our children need them (you can find out more about this in my book *The Powerful Proactive Parent's Guide to Present Parenting*)

In a nutshell, how responsive we are to their needs and how we provide for those needs before they need them helps them to feel loved, safe, and content. This way, they know they are loved and cared for and that they are special. This sense of security is like the snuggliest comfort blanket we can provide as parents. When our children trust us to be there for them and support their needs, they learn to trust others, and life. This builds their self-esteem and confidence because they know we've got their back no matter what.

Our job as parents is to equip our children with the survival skills to go it alone and fly the nest one day. If we don't support them with this, then who will?

It may be hard to imagine now while you're nursing a new-born, that one day, sooner than you think, they will be an adolescent or adult leaving home, embarking on this adventure called life, all alone without you.

What we all hope as parents is that they remember the good advice that we've given them, the morals and common sense and initiative we have instilled over the years so when we are not present, they will hear our voice in their head, guiding them positively in any life changing decisions they make.

What we don't want is for them to do what pleases us or live the life which we wish we had lived, or make the same mistakes as us. But, in our attempts to avoid these pitfalls, we may inadvertently do just that. You see, they will hear your voice in their head every time they make a decision, but they may confuse it with their own choice.

Our children need to feel competent and to also feel good about themselves and their abilities, but when they are very young and learning (this often means making mistakes because that's how all of us learn best), we tend to try to help them by showing them what they've done wrong and telling them off, we only do this because we don't want them to repeat things that could negatively affect their health and safety, but what actually happens is we unintentionally end up making them feel bad or as though they've failed, leaving them doubting themselves and their abilities. When we praise them for their efforts rather than achievements, we let them know we are proud of them and make them more inclined to keep trying regardless of any failures or mistakes, believing they can succeed eventually. If we tell them off for mistakes, they won't want to try again through fear or disapproval, judgement, and feeling like they can't do it.

We don't want to do everything for our children, they have to learn how to do things for themselves if they are to feel self-confident and have a good level of self-esteem. They learn from doing and being involved, not watching other people doing.

When we are overly anxious about our children trying new things or making mistakes, or when we don't give them the respect they deserve, we hinder their developmental progress to be independent, self-confident people with high self-esteem.

There is a saying that 'children should respect their elders.' But respect is earnt, not an automatic right once we reach a certain age. If we want our children to respect us, then we show them how by being respectful toward them, and this respect starts from birth.

It's easy to assume that a tiny baby doesn't require respect the same way another adult would, but this is not the case. When caring for a baby, we can show respect not just in the way we approach their care, but how we explain to them beforehand what it is we are going 'to do' to them. Yes, when we change their nappies, bathe them or pass them to a friend for a cuddle, we need to let them know this is what we intend to do to them (they have no choice what's done to them, and they can't do for themselves) beforehand, this is proactively preparing them in advance. Now they may not understand the exact words you are saying, but having this interaction beforehand doesn't feel like they are being thrust into a situation.

For example, Aunty Ann has come to visit and can't wait for a cuddle with baby Joy. Baby Joy is kicking about in her Moses basket having fun when Aunty Ann reaches in and picks her up with no word of warning. Baby Joy may not be very familiar with Aunty Ann but even if she is, this is not the way to ask for a cuddle. A better approach would be for Joy's Mummy to introduce Aunty Ann to Joy by saying 'Look who's come to see you, Joy, its Aunty Ann.' Then for Aunty Ann to approach the Moses basket with a warm, welcoming smile as she introduces herself and asks if she can have a cuddle.

This way, Joy will reciprocate if she is old enough with a smile, as babies love to mimic adults, and she will want to get to know and be cuddled by Aunty Ann. Here, there's a mutual respect where both people feel good about the interaction.

The same goes for when we are about to change a nappy or give them a bath, explaining beforehand and taking our time, not rushing and using sudden movements, helps a baby feel at ease. We are constantly communicating with our children, even when we are not using any words, so it's important to make that communication as positive as we possibly can. Especially in the first eight years of life when they are developing their concept of self and who they are, as this programming will mould the adult they are likely to become. Our babies don't understand we have anything else in our lives to be doing other than being with them, they still think they are part of us and they are the centre of the universe.

When we impatiently rush through another nappy change, they are feeling; I'm not worthy of your time. They are not thinking this on a conscious, intellectual level, it's a feeling, so the experience either feels good to them or not. They are not comprehending that we have a million and one other urgent things to be doing. It's rather black and white for babies, there's no shades of grey that can justify anything else other than good or not good.

When we are carrying out caring routines, we need to be mindful of how that experience is feeling for our baby or child, good or not good is the only measure.

How we interact and play with our children really does have a lasting impact on them. Impressions begin in the womb, not when they are old enough to understand and talk. They are building pictures of themselves in their mind from day one, let's hope we help them paint a positive one.

The odd rushed nappy here and there, or odd time we get stressed out and shout at them, is not going to cause an irreversible, damaging effect upon them that they'll never get over. We are all human, and its normal to behave like one, none of us are perfect parents. Pretending our children are always perfect and taking the softly, softly approach and walking on eggshells around them is not going to help them build resilience in the real world either, so a degree of reality is important. But it's the constant, repetitive impatience, lack of time and consideration for them and put downs, nagging and shouting, or physical punishments that leave long term emotional scars that although not physically seen, are apparent in how our children behave and who they become. Our time and patience are what gives our children self-worth, but both of these can be in short supply at times, creating habits and routines in our daily lives are what prevents those 'at times' becoming 'all the time.'

3 HAPPY THINGS

When my children were younger, each night before bed, I would ask them to think of three things that they were happy for in their day. Discussing the good things that have happened in their day while tucking them into bed helps aid in a restful night's sleep. Children want to chat at bedtime, so using this time to find out what they enjoyed doing, what went well, and what made them feel happy, helps them to drift off to dream world, remembering all that's good about life. And that one nightly habit not only keeps our children grateful and focused on the positives, but creates daily Us Time that we may not have had the time to give them that day.

THE BOTHER BOX

It can be hard to turn off fears and negative thoughts, so children may start to talk about what's bothering them and what didn't go well in their day, this is important to address, but do you think if it was really bothering them, they would wait until bedtime to tell you?

It's true, worries and fears do surface in the dark, still, quiet of night, and lots of children are scared of the dark, but we don't want our children to dwell on all the bad stuff at bedtime. We are better off distracting them if possible and shifting to the positive parts of their day while reassuring them that in the morning, we will discuss the things that are bothering them when we can take action to do something about them.

A good way to do this and to prevent worries building up or going unaddressed is by creating a 'Bother Box'. This ensures they feel they always have a place to put their concerns. When they have created the 'bother box' they will have a place to put all their bothers into so they don't build up in their head. For this find an old shoebox and ask your child to decorate their box as they choose with paint, crayons, or stickers. Buy a pack of copier paper, and each time they feel bothered by something, encourage them to draw a picture of whatever is bothering them and place it in the box. Then, once a week, maybe as part of Us Time, you can take the time to sit down together and go through the concerns in the box. When they have an outlet for their bothersome thoughts, such as drawing a picture of them, and they are placed in the bother box, they are out of their head and in the box ready to be addressed with someone they love and trust. As they get older, they can exchange drawing pictures for writing their worries down on post it notes, then when they get to their teens, they will already be in the habit of managing their thoughts and discussing their concerns with you, until they progress onto a journal and diary where they can work through them themselves. Yes, there will come a point when they won't want to share all their worries or problems with their parents, partly because some of these they will believe are due to their parents ruining their life and stopping them having fun.

I'm sure you can relate to your own teenage injustices too?

I can still remember a four-page rant I wrote as a teen when my Father wouldn't let me go to a Glastonbury Music Festival. I just couldn't believe how unfair he was for keeping me away from all the fun I could have had in a muddy field!

I mean, there seemed little point discussing it further with him, so my diary was the next best thing. I read it and laugh now, decades later, hopefully, your child will too. So, don't ever feel upset if they won't let you in or read their personal diaries slating you in the future, be glad they have a place to vent and get it out of their head. Yes, they are probably wrong, as I was, but they have to work that out for themselves!

As proactive parents, we want to keep our children safe and to prevent our children's unwanted thoughts and feelings from getting out of control. Left to their own devices, they can run wild. Emotions, once they get a grip, can be too strong to control. By addressing how our children are thinking and feeling before there's an obvious issue, we prevent strong, unpleasant feelings or a negative, automatic thought-cycle taking hold.

Giving our children tools and techniques such as the 'bother box' or playing the 'As If' game, using 'affirmations' and recounting 'three happy things' in their day, gives them coping mechanisms and preventative tools to cope, before they need them.

As a society, we don't tend to address our children's mental health until it really demands attention, at this point, we are usually quite late in the intervention process. Especially when it comes to anxiety. We think they'll get over it, grow out of it, etc... but it builds and builds until it becomes an explosive, volatile, emotional bomb, too hot for us to handle!

But we can't combat our children's emotions such as anger with being angry ourselves, that only throws fuel onto an already blazing fire. The only approach that will remedy unwelcome emotions is love.

Love dissolves worry, therefore, giving our love freely and unconditionally is the remedy to most problems, and it's the core of creating a high level of self-esteem in our children, which is why it's such a significant part of the U URSELF Routine, and one aspect we'll lovingly uncover next.

CHAPTER 8:
LOVE—BONDED BY
UNCONDITIONAL LOVE

Love is the greatest gift, the strongest force there is,
It gives the highest lift, to those who fly with it,
Love is easy when times are hard,
It guides the spirit, through the good and the bad,
Love is always truthful, it cannot tell lies,
It brings us people to love, and it takes them back with goodbyes.

—*Emma Grant*

LOVE IS THE FOUNDATION

THE U URSELF ROUTINE includes all the ingredients our children need to be happy, healthy, and successful.

But out of them all, love is the main one.

In the absence of love, children fail to thrive.

Love forms the basis of the whole recipe, that's why it needs to be routinely given as part of the U URSELF Routine.

There's no doubt you are a loving parent, the fact you are taking the time to read this book proves you love and care. But you don't have anything to prove, love is naturally present all the time in all of us. Life just sometimes clouds how we display love. When we are busy, stressed, and struggling to keep it all together, we can make love conditional.

My Nan taught me unconditional love, she brought me up as a child, and I wrote the poem in this opening chapter to read at her funeral and had part of it transcribed on her headstone.

She was the epitome of a real-life walking, talking, caring, feeling, unconditional source, of endless, selfless, overflowing love. And I aspired to be like her and pass on her loving essence in my own parenting role.

And indeed, this book was born from my desire to pass on all she taught me about being an unconditionally loving parent.

WHAT IS YOUR IDEA OF A LOVING PARENT?

The Oxford popular dictionary describes a parent as; N. Father or Mother; Ancestor; Source from which other things are derived.

But that is too basic a definition, a parent is a lot more than that.

We need to know what our definition of a parent is and how we see ourselves in relation to that. Knowing this enables us to identify where we need to focus more or less of our attention as a parent.

The following questions may help, and you'll find it useful to write your answers down to reflect back upon.

Don't try to censor any thought; our idea about what the word parent means to us is very personal.

Depending on our own relationship with our own parents, the word parent could have positive or negative connotations.

- Given the choice, would you have chosen your parents to be your parents?
- Why would/wouldn't you have chosen them?
- Given a choice, do you think your child would have chosen you as their parent?
- Why would/wouldn't they have chosen you do you think?
- What image does the word 'Parent' bring to mind, and what feelings does it produce?
- Do those images or feelings correspond with how we act as a parent or not?
- If they do, in what way?
- If they don't, how or why don't they?
- What words best describe what a loving parent is?

171

This exercise probably raised some emotional memories and feelings, bringing to light how your parents were with you. This may be very different to how you feel you should or shouldn't be with your own children. As pleasant or painful as this exercise may be, those thoughts and feelings are useful in helping us to become the loving parent we want to be.

HOW DO YOU THINK A LOVING PARENT SHOULD BE?

There are no right or wrong answers to this question. It just depends on our personal opinions and experience.

But here's a list of some words that could be used to describe a typical loving parent:

- Loving
- Kind
- Caring
- Considerate
- Coach
- Protective
- Understanding
- Teacher
- Selfless
- Knowledgeable
- Trustworthy
- Honest
- Supportive
- Patient
- Playful
- Proactive
- Positive Role model
- Generous
- Genuine
- Thoughtful

- Forgiving
- Faithful
- Present
- Devoted
- Friend
- Counsellor
- Committed
- Giving
- Available
- Engaging
- Attentive
- Accepting
- Affectionate
- Encouraging
- Unconditional
- Warm

What word/words stood out for you?

Those words can give you an idea of what it is you most want to be like with your children. When we are aware of what kind of a parent we would most like to be, we can become that way and notice when we are not.

Let's take the last word on the list 'Warm'.

This is a good word to describe a loving parent. It encompasses the role nicely because the word 'warm' or 'warmth' means welcoming, inviting, cosy, loving, enthusiastic, affectionate, hearty, and kindly.

A warm person is glad to see us, and we are glad to see them too. They can light up a room with their presence. Everyone wants to be with or around them because warm people genuinely love. People can feel their heat radiating out toward them, full of positive, calming energy. It's a quality every child is drawn to and can easily warm to.

WARM UP EXERCISE

- Go through the previous example of words to describe a loving parent again and think of ways to become more welcoming, loving, enthusiastic, affectionate, understanding, kind, and so on.
- What could we do or say today to demonstrate each example to our children? Could we be more understanding the next time they wet the bed or more generous with Us Time?
- Can't think right now of anything you could do or say to your child? Then just imagine someone else you know/knew who you consider being a warm person with the above qualities and imagine how they would demonstrate being a loving parent. How would they act toward their child in similar situations to you? Write those thoughts down, then practice trying out their approach on your child. Noticing if you get warmer in the process or whether your child warms more to you as a result.

WHY IS IT SO IMPORTANT?

Love is the crutch all children rely on. It stands by them and supports them when they make mistakes as well as celebrating their achievements.

Open, unconditional love plays a major factor in helping children deal with changes in their life, good or bad, and in assisting them with transitions, such as starting school.

Children who feel loved physically and emotionally, feel secure and love themselves, as well as others.

When we form positive, loving relationships with our children while young, we help them form those kinds of relationships with others, both now and later on in life. Helping them to grow up empathetic, understanding, secure, and caring adults.

This way, they won't look to others to fill them up with love, but look to share their love instead. Love gives children the confidence to be themselves.

Every child's true nature is to be loving and lovable, they are born oozing love from every pore, expecting to be loved equally.

The latter 'loved' is the part we play in helping them to realize their own true nature. In return, they make us feel loved, loving, and lovable, a powerful threesome in any relationship.

But first, we need to learn how to love ourselves before we can truly love or teach our children about love.

LEARNING TO LOVE YOURSELF

There's a true saying:

'If you don't love yourself, then who will?'

We must look after and love ourselves, mistakes, imperfections and all.

If there's something we don't love about ourselves, then others may not love that aspect of us either.

Not because it's not lovable, but because we will transmit the message of how we feel about ourselves to other people that we meet.

Our partners may think we are beautiful, but if we think we are ugly, over time, we will start to dress and look the way we feel.

Self-love shouldn't be reliant on others loving us though.

We should replace any damaging, empty, unhealthy relationship with another, for a more meaningful, loving relationship with ourselves.

Getting to know who we really are as individuals is self-love. The relationship we have with ourselves influences all the other relationships in our lives, and our love for ourselves is more important than any other love we may, or may not, receive from others.

Fat, thin, rich, poor, happy, or depressed, it makes no odds; you can love yourself regardless of who you think you are, or however your past may have been.

Loving yourself does not need to depend on past or future events or relationships. Anyone can start afresh today and learn to love themselves, no matter what.

It's the single most loving thing we can do for our children.

We are their greatest asset in life, so we must take good care of our own health and happiness. Should we become ill, we would not be in a position to care for them. Surely If only to keep us in a strong position to take care of our children at all times, that's all the motivation we need to ensure we love and care for ourselves?

We need to learn to love ourselves the same way we love our children. To help with this, let's try the following exercise.

LOVING YOURSELF THROUGH YOUR CHILD'S EYES EXERCISE

Close your eyes for a moment now. Then imagine your child in the future, grown up as a parent themselves with their own child.

How do you see them?

Can you see, hear, or feel them as a kind, caring, gentle, relaxed, patient, and loving parent toward their own child?

Can you hear them enjoying their life, laughing with and loving others?

Are they;

A responsible adult and parent with honesty and integrity? Healthy, happy calm, relaxed, patient, optimistic, and fulfilled?

Making time for themselves and taking care of how they look, spending money that they have worked for on themselves and others?

In a career they love. Smart, successful, and abundant while being humble, content, and grateful?

Or are they;

Angry, worried, stressed, sad, frustrated, or depressed, struggling to make ends meet and sacrificing their time on the needs of everyone else?

What would you like them to look, sound, and feel like as a parent?

Imagine now that you are their child. What do you want for them as your parent? Love, happiness, abundance, and peace of mind?

Can you feel this overwhelming love, respect, and admiration for them as your parent?

Do you look up to them and aspire to be like them when you grow up?

See them as the parent, putting their arms around you as their child. Listen as they wish you all the good that you have wished for them.

Open your eyes now and be their parent again. The parent your child wants you to be and the parent you wish your child will become in the future.

When we love ourselves the way we love our children, we become a living, loving example. (Or a living example of love.)

When they see us loving and caring for ourselves and addressing our own needs, they reap the benefits of our happiness, and it teaches them how to love and treat themselves.

As parents, we often go without in life to give our children a better standard of living. This is second nature and seems the right, admirable thing to do, but this can sometimes make our children feel uncomfortable.

How can they enjoy anything that results in a lack for the one that they love?

I know my Nan made sacrifices for me, and looking back, this makes me feel sad because she's no longer here, but I'm enjoying an abundant, happy life. I feel she should have given herself more of her love, time, and money. We are all here on a separate journey, sharing experiences together, but we are all responsible for creating our own lives and making our own future.

LOVE IS IN THE MOMENT

Being a loving parent is not something that we have to learn or change about ourselves.

It's not something we do or do not have; it's who we are, or who we are not.

We don't do something in particular to suddenly become a loving parent, we just are loving at that moment or not. We have the choice.

It's the same for anything else we want to change, just because we are angry at our children for something they have done, doesn't make us an angry, unloving parent. An hour later we may be praising them and showering them with love.

Our behaviours and emotions change from moment to moment.

As long as we are aware of them, we can be the loving parents that deep down we all are, through our conscious moment to moment choices.

But we can't decide to be a loving parent one day and that's it, we can never get angry or upset ever again.

That would be acting something that we are not, and suppressing or denying our true feelings is pointless as emotions always manifest in one way or another eventually.

It's best to allow ourselves to be and feel as we choose, but not to think that is who we are, or that we can't change.

Moment by moment, we can all change and be the loving parent we choose to be, regardless of our past actions or behaviour.

The way we act is transparent to children, they may not always question us on a conscious level, but deep down, they know and understand our true feelings.

We can't act one way and say something else or say something and act differently. Our actions need to correspond with our words. We need to physically demonstrate our love and reaffirm it with words daily.

Love given unconditionally is returned tenfold. There's no better feeling than when our children tell us they love us. It uplifts, motivates, inspires, comforts, and gives us that warm fuzzy feeling inside known as unconditional love.

UNCONDITIONAL LOVE

There's no reward, praise, gift, good behaviour, or anything else we can expect, better than that.

Anything other than unconditional love will feel like hard work because it usually relies on our children meeting our expectations, which is always going to be difficult.

Unconditional love means that no matter what our children do or don't do, say or don't say, it doesn't affect the love that we feel for them. Even when we feel as though they've let us down, those are the best moments to practice unconditional love, and there will be many of them. When our children need discipline, this may seem the hardest time to give them our love, but it's the time they need it most.

If they say, 'I hate you,' we can counteract it with 'I love you.'

If they do something wrong, we can give them a cuddle instead of telling them off while we explain right from wrong lovingly.

It's not about overlooking what they do wrong, letting them have their own way, or giving in to them. It's about freeing ourselves to love unconditionally so that everyone feels good. You'll know the difference between naturally occurring, unconditional love, and trying to force love. Anything other than the former will be a constant, tiring, struggle, making us feel, guilty, anxious, drained, angry, frustrated, or unhappy.

Love is all that ever matters in our relationship with our children. Nothing else is as important as unconditional love, ever. If it feels like hard work, then it's not unconditional love. If we are trying to restrict, control, or have a hold on or over our children, it's conditional love. It feels like we are enduring our parenting role. We need not endure unconditional love, but enjoy it. It's a freedom. It's an allowing. It's a letting go.

When we are unconditionally loving parents, then we will have equally loving children. Being loving satisfies a basic need within all of us.

Once we realise that our children are neither good nor bad, they are just being themselves in each and every moment, and we can stop judging them, we can then truly love them unconditionally. From this unconditional loving position, we no longer need to excuse our children's behaviour or feel embarrassed by it.

It's only a form of self-expression at that moment, and it's okay.

We want them to love themselves, but if they feel bad or naughty all the time, they'll find it hard to do this, wondering what's wrong with them.

But there's absolutely nothing wrong with them, how could there be—they originate from a source of love.

When we accept and approve of them, they will accept and approve of themselves. Making them more inclined to respect others and less inclined to hurt, humiliate, or compete with others.

ENCOURAGING THE FLOW OF LOVE

We will always feel loving, loved, and lovable when we surround ourselves only with people and things that we love.

As babies, we love everything, even the ordinary is extraordinary.

Yet, somewhere along the line, as we learn to compartmentalise and realise what things are and what they do, we lose our love. It's as though the magic is lost.

The secret is to start to notice love and appreciate it all again.

Even the neglected old dried out potted plant in the corner and the junk in the drawer.

If we don't, then we are going to let it go and release it to someone who will give it the love and attention that it deserves. Leaving us only with those things that we love.

When we are surrounded by love, it flows freely to others.

FOR LOVE NOT MONEY

Releasing the unloved, material things in life can encourage our children to love and appreciate what they have more.

Love is priceless, so no matter how many possessions we lavish our children with, they can never compensate for our love or time.

If children constantly want materialistic things but are never satisfied, no matter what they have, they could be craving love and trying to fill that void with possessions that they don't really want or need.

By actually listening to their reasons why they feel the need for something and saying 'no' to their demands for more things, we are carrying out an act of love.

We are better off focusing on our daily loving quota than spending our money on toys. The more we have to spend, the more we have to earn and work, meaning less time with our children.

We can add up the love we give our children instead of the gifts. Keeping a journal and recording the three most loving things we've done for our children each day helps us keep score.

Everything we do for our children is an act of love, so the lists will be endless. Listing only three things is plenty though to prove to ourselves of all the love we already give and to alleviate any guilt we may have over what we don't do or give.

A good example would be:

1. Cooked a homemade Shepherd's pie for dinner.
2. Read a bedtime story.
3. Listened to each child individually discuss their day at school.

Those things all mean more than money or possessions.

Love equals Time, and that's the most loving investment we can make in our children's lives. We can always buy more stuff, but we can never buy more time. Once spent, it's gone forever. Love in the moment. This moment is all that counts. And all those loving moments soon add up.

BONDED BY LOVE

It's those everyday acts of love such as cooking tea and chatting about their day that strengthens the bond we share with our children.

Expressing our love a little longer than expected reinforces our love.

Next time, try hugging your child a couple of minutes longer than usual and feel the love transmitted back and forth. That's our bonds strengthening and reconnecting us to one another.

Sometimes, stuff happens in life, and we may find ourselves parted from our children, whether through work, divorce, illness, or whatever else.

In those circumstances it's vital we look for ways to get back together as soon as possible and reconnect, repairing any bonds.

If not, our children could look elsewhere for comfort and support and may turn to the wrong people or pastimes in our absence.

As parents, we sometimes worry that we won't get parenting right. Believing that someone else such as a partner, grandparent, aunty, foster carer, child-minder, nursery worker, or teacher will do a better job of loving or raising our children the right way.

The truth is, no one could ever do a better job than you can at loving your child.

It's not what happens in life that's the problem, it's how we choose to deal with what happens.

Problems and disagreements are part and parcel of parenting, which we can't eliminate, but we can learn how to deal with and overcome them.

Offering a reassuring hug, kiss, or smile is all it takes to repair a kink in the chain of love that connects us.

Disagreements will always occur in loving relationships, but if we take action to resolve things as soon as possible and are willing and able to work through issues with our children, we strengthen our bonds.

We can't just set aside an hour a day as part of the U URSELF routine to show our children how much we love them, then forget to maintain that connection for the other twenty-three hours of the day.

It's constant connections that keep bonds strong.

Work, bills, and other daily worries won't disappear. They will always be there demanding our attention, but without time and energy, those loving bonds could gradually start to dissolve over time.

The good news is, bonds are harder to break than they are to make, and fortunately, being related instantly bonds us to our children. It just takes a little time and effort to keep it going strong.

If unrelated biologically to our children, a little more groundwork and effort in creating that bond may be necessary. As they will try and test our love to establish if we genuinely care about them or not. While they are testing us, or whenever they push us away as we try to connect with them, if we can practice setting aside any emotions or rejection we may feel and are patient, we will finally gain their trust. Then we can create a bond as good as, if not stronger than a biological child and parent.

It's a choice to love a child that you didn't give birth to, a choice you don't have to commit to. When you give birth to your own child, love is just expected. Any child that we choose to care and love for that is not biologically ours, will come to respect and appreciate that choice, more so than a birth child who would naturally take our love for granted.

WHAT IF LOVE IS ABSENT?

As parents, we're expected to bond instantly with our children, but this isn't always the case.

It's not love at first sight for all parents, and unconditional love is not always automatically present. It's not that it's not there somewhere, it's just that it's been overshadowed by trauma. Any physical or emotional illness that either ourselves or our children have experienced, or a difficult pregnancy or birth, can initially get in the way of the bonding process.

Insensitive, somewhat helpful friends and family may try to reassure us or question our feelings toward our children, often making us feel worse. Leaving us feeling abnormal or guilty that we should act or feel a certain way.

No one will ever understand how we feel until they feel the same.

It's scary stuff being a parent, the level of responsibility is immense. But the fact that we are even worried about how we feel, is a strong sign that we care a lot about our children.

Instead of hiding feelings out of guilt, shame or embarrassment, reach out, there's always help available when we are open, receptive, and willing to find it. Join parenting or support groups, or alternatively, talk to your GP for further help. When you talk about things with others, you'll be surprised to find you're not alone in how you feel.

Unconditional love is a feeling and not a thing that is always within and available to us. At some point, everyone experiences dark times that overshadow the light of love. But love grows or diminishes, depending on the contribution that is made to it.

Romantic love gives the false illusion that we should just feel in love with someone all of the time. That's why so many people fall out of love with their partners, they either set too many conditions, or they stop putting in the effort to keep their love alive.

We can't, however, just fall out of love with our children the same way we would a partner and find new ones when we've had enough of ours.

Likewise, our children can't just leave us and find new parents if we fall out with them, so we have to care and love one another, no matter what.

IT'S NEVER TOO LATE TO LOVE

It's never too late to love. I myself after being parted from my Mother for many years as a child, re-established a bond with my Mother as a teenager. We can all establish or reconnect those bonds with our children or parents by building those bridges and being the first to reach out and forgive.

Every thought that we think about our children or every action or inaction we take creates our relationship with them. The amount of time and energy we invest in our children shows them how much we love and value them. But it's not just what we do, it's how we do it too. Parenting is just like cooking. If we put the right ingredients in, at the right time, mix together, and lovingly watch over them patiently, we create an alchemical delight that fulfils us.

Despite providing our children with food, sleep, shelter, exercise, recreation, and education, without love, the dish is incomplete, and it's not an ingredient that can easily be added at a later date. Try adding a raw clove of garlic to your meal after its been cooked, and you'll undoubtedly be left with a bad taste in your mouth.

Love has many forms of expression, and the following chapter and final part of the U URSELF Routine, Food, is another expression of that love.

CHAPTER 9:
FOOD—MAKING A MEAL
OF MEALTIMES

FOOD FOR THOUGHT

W E HAVE COME TO the final part in the U URSELF Routine—Food. This chapter will give us plenty of food for thought. But we don't want to make a meal out of it. We want to create a calm approach to the usual mealtime mayhem, so the main emphasis will be on making mealtimes an enjoyable experience for everyone.

There are three courses in this chapter, for starters, our children's nutritional needs, then for the main, eating habits, and finally, creating a positive mealtime experience, making the issue of food sweeter for everyone to swallow.

Children's eating habits vary, some bolt food down without chewing, others stare at food in horror as if it's infused with deadly arsenic.

Eating habits are also influenced by preferences, including tastes and textures, the quantity needed, and the times they eat, along with each child's activity levels.

This makes mealtimes stressful, as we worry whether they are eating the right type of food, in the right quantity, at the right time.

But we don't want to make a meal out of it, as it's equally stressful for our children when we become obsessional over their eating habits.

Food is a source of pleasure as much as a basic necessity; picnics in the park, fish and chips on the beach, birthday parties, Sunday roasts, dinning out, takeaways, holiday buffets, school dinners, and tea at a friend's house all are sociable, enjoyable occasions.

Food equals love, comfort, necessity, and pleasure all in one, but too much of a good thing can be bad.

NUTRITIONAL NEEDS

It's a mystery trying to decipher the jargon on food packets, and often, we just don't have the time. It's worth taking a course or reading a few books on nutrition though, as what we think is healthy or low fat often isn't. Children need at least five portions of fruit and vegetables a day, and a good balance of fibre, protein, fat, and carbohydrates to be healthy. Yes, our children do need fat such as those found in meat, poultry, nuts, margarine, butter and milk. Polyunsaturated fats are the omega 3 and 6 good fats found in olive oil and oily fish, monounsaturated fats can be found naturally in red meat or avocados. Then we have the bad fats, the artificially created Trans fats found in chocolate, snacks and fried food, those are the ones to be avoided.

The main thing is providing an overall balanced diet. Food's main purpose is to provide energy and nutrients. Nutrients are; proteins, carbohydrates, fats, minerals, and vitamins. Offering foods that are rich in calcium, such as yoghurt, cheese, and milk, iron found in eggs and red meat, and protein from fish, or beans, pulses, and nuts if they are vegetarian, should ensure they are healthy, along with appropriately sized, regular meals.

When it comes to food, fresh is best and homemade healthiest.

If we cook and prepare everything ourselves from fresh produce, avoid anything that comes in a box, packet, or tin, we can't go far wrong.

Cooking from scratch may be a little time consuming, yet it's often cheaper in the long run than ready meals or takeouts. Cooking up batches of meals in advance and chilling or freezing them so we have convenient, healthy, homemade ready meals available throughout the week, is a good idea.

One afternoon in the kitchen with a few key ingredients can supply a weeks' worth of dinners, improving our families' health and finance, as well as saving time. It's also a way of passing on traditions and offering comfort.

TRADITION

Comfort food is aptly named so because it's associated with childhood, which holds memories of being young, loved, safe, healthy, and cared for.

Many memories and traditions are associated with comforting food. Parents through the generations still pass down secret family recipes, and the traditional Sunday roast is a classic, family favourite that hopefully will never go out of fashion.

Comforting, hearty, homemade roasts, soups, or stews, can all nurture and nourish inside and out.

Preparing the meals ourselves means we know exactly what goes into the food our children eat.

The main benefits of homemade meals include having control over wholesome ingredients and additives, knowing there's no hidden nasty salt or sugar, preservatives, or hydrogenated fats. But as cooking a meal for your family to eat is an act of love, you can also put your love into it, and those you love will appreciate your efforts.

Tradition and food are strongly linked. Occasions such as Pancake Day educate and help children become aware of annual traditions or religious beliefs. It can also help them to understand the time and days of the week, such as it must be Friday because we are having fish and chips.

JUNK VERSES HEALTHY EATING

As parents, we have the power to create a junk food junkie or health food fanatic because we provide the food they eat.

There's no argument concerning which type of food is best, the clue 'junk' and 'healthy' are in the name. Both are just habits. Healthy eating is a habit as much as unhealthy eating is, the more we feed one, the bigger and stronger it becomes, as so do our children.

If children are often ill or tired all the time, then their diet should be one of the first things to be taken into consideration. Lacking in energy could be due to nutritional deficiencies or not consuming enough calories for their needs.

Energy comes from the food that they eat, and generally, they need more food the more energetic they are. A busy day full of activity will be reflected in increased appetite, or a quiet relaxing day means they'll want and need less food. The type of food they eat will also affect their energy levels.

Occasional treats are okay. They remove temptation or compulsion to want them. What they're allowed, they won't crave, but when we forbid them, they want them more, remember Adam and Eve and that apple?

Dentists recommend choosing one treat day a week, eating sweets all in one go, then brushing their teeth afterward. This is better than slowly consuming sweets throughout the day, allowing sugar to linger and stick to their teeth, causing decay.

CHANGES IN FOOD HABITS

The problem is today, sweet and salty treats are no longer a treat. They are more of an everyday habit.

This adds unnecessary, excess calories to our children's daily diet, and with less and less outdoor physical activity now the norm, our children are not able to burn off all those excess calories.

Having adequate recreational exercise as part of their U URSELF Routine will help manage their weight. But we can't blame our children's size or weight on lack of physical exercise alone.

Calorie consumption in certain foods and drink is exceptionally high these days and sold in larger portion sizes. Changes over the last fifty years, means that our convenient lifestyles are having a negative impact on weight and overall health. This will affect children now and for the rest of their lives as adults. Vast amounts of money are made from the fast food industry, resulting in serious health consequences. These people who produce and sell convenient, processed, junk food, don't care about our children's health. They believe we should control and regulate our children's diets.

This is true, it's our responsibility, but they don't make it easy for us.

Our innocent children have been born into fast food and know no other way unless we show them.

They see their friends eating junk, and the cool adverts on TV, and we buy the food for them, so they believe it must be okay to eat it.

We are led to believe it's normal to eat processed food because it's everywhere, and everyone's doing it. Yet supermarkets still sell cigarettes, but we know they kill, so that's not a good enough excuse to overlook the problem.

Every day, our children are consuming empty, excess calories in large amounts from sugary drinks like fizzy pop and fruit juices. Water may be the boring option, but it's the most essential drink to rehydrate and give them the energy, focus, and concentration they need. We have a current obesity epidemic due to all the processed food, snacks, and sugar, now a normal part of our children's daily diet. Food companies have powerful food advertising campaigns and fast food is convenient, cheap, and available twenty-four seven. No need to even go out and get it, it can be delivered straight to our door, ready to eat.

The supermarket is also designed to make us buy things we don't need. Essentials like bread are usually strategically placed at the back of the store, so we have to pass tempting, buy one get one free snacks. The bag of apples is never buy one get one free though, that's because we won't get addicted to apples, they are healthy and nutritious, but biscuits, sweets or crisps are addictive, empty calories full of fat, salt, and sugar with no nutritional benefits. When we buy two multi-bags of crisps or chocolate, we eat twice as much, faster, in larger quantities, and end up replacing them. The more we buy, the more we eat and the more we eat, the more we buy, well they are free? Shopping online can keep us focused and never shopping when hungry or without a list helps.

As an experiment, to check how addicted your children are to these unhealthy foods, empty all the food cupboards, fridges and freezers of all junk food. Either throw it out or give it away to those in need and see how your children react to the replacement of healthier options, such as fruit.

HUNGER STRIKE

Healthier options can lead to a hunger strike, but we must persevere.

Once they see we won't give in to their food demands, they will eventually give in and eat what we want them to eat, even if they have to endure a few days of hunger strike first.

We needn't worry, they won't starve. We often forget about the breakfast cereal, toast, yoghurt, and odd snacks here and there or drinks they are having.

The only concern we should have when trying to overcome fussy eating is that we have chosen a time when WE are feeling good, physically and mentally.

We have to commit to staying focused and strong to cope with their behaviour and demands. Because when children don't eat properly, they get tired, irritable, and misbehave.

We can't get overemotional if they refuse to eat the Casserole we've lovingly cooked them. And we certainly shouldn't be tempted to give them chicken nuggets instead because they refuse to eat it.

If we do, they will come to expect their preferred alternative all the time. Not because they prefer the chicken nuggets to the casserole, but because they will have learnt how to get their own way. You can throw the casserole in the bin if they refuse to eat it, but never give them anything else. If they are not hungry or refuse to eat, simply clear it away and wait until their next meal.

As long as we don't allow them to snack unhealthily in the meantime, they will soon associate their refusal to eat dinner with hunger, serving as a good reminder to eat their next meal and giving them an appetite.

Explaining to them in a relaxed manner, that the food is there if they are hungry and want it, gives them a choice.

Once they realize they have the choice to eat it or not, and it doesn't bother us either way, then, if hungry, they will eat it.

You may not think it can be this simple and you may have tried unsuccessfully in the past, but perseverance is key. I know it works as it's a method I've seen work with lots of children over the years over and over again, in fact, I've never known it to fail unless parents have given up before they've given it a real go.

We have to mean what we say though and say what we mean, calmly and confidently. Such as, 'The food's there if you are hungry, if not, you don't have to eat it, but there will be nothing else to eat.'

They might say they are hungry but don't like what we are offering them, but we mustn't feel guilty for doing the right thing, they have a choice.

If we keep offering casserole day in, day out, with no other option, and we never blackmail or force them to eat it, eventually, they will eat it. Some parents protest their children would never eat casserole, but they never persevere long enough to find out, especially if they dislike it themselves.

Casserole is not a punishment, its love in a bowl.

By providing healthy, nutritious meals, we have nothing to feel guilty about.

Likewise, children should not be made to feel guilty for not eating either, despite our efforts or concerns.

Our Children are not concerned that we have spent hours slaving over a hot stove, spent a fortune on the best organic ingredients, or created a culinary piece of art.

So, we can forget trying to make them feel guilty for our labour, this only adds to their obstinate nature.

They can't contemplate the future either and don't understand it when we say:

'If you don't eat now, you'll be hungry later'

They can't think that far ahead about how they might feel later. They think and feel at the moment they are in. That's why feeling hungry is a good way of demonstrating the consequences of not eating their meal.

FUSSY EATER

All children go through phases though, and fussy eating is just one of those phases.

One-day, Macaroni Cheese is their favourite and they want it every day, the next, Spaghetti Bolognaise becomes the flavour of the month. Children like to keep eating what they love most, it's comforting and familiar.

We don't need to stress about it, faddy eaters never stick to one thing forever, that's why they are called fads. Neophobia (the fear of anything new) is when babies and young children fear new food. It's a common, developmental stage for under three's, but if we pander to this, it will remain with them a lifetime.

Avoiding the feared food perpetuates their anxiety in the future. We can avoid this by offering them a wide variety of foods from a young age, and instead of removing foods that cause them anxiety, offer those foods more often and keep re-introducing them. Even if they refuse a particular food, persevere, their tastes change often. So, keep offering new or disliked foods alongside foods they like, and eventually, when in the mood, they'll try them.

If they don't, at least they will still have something else to eat that they do like. Not liking certain foods does not make them a fussy eater; it could be certain foods do not appeal to their taste buds at that time, that's not to say they never will. Children's refusal to eat could be their ever-changing pallet or a normal part of flexing their independence. Exercising their freedom of choice, they may decide not to like a certain food anymore, particularly if they sense our anxiety over them refusing to eat, or they gain attention.

If we make a fuss over their fussy eating, they get what they're seeking, undue attention. Our mealtime mantra should be, 'No fuss at mealtimes', unless we want a fussy eater.

Our job as a loving parent is done when we have prepared and plated up a nutritious meal. The rest is up to them, no need to insist, beg, or force feed them to eat. We can't eat it for them or make them chew or swallow food, it's their choice whether they want to eat it or not. It's not giving in to them, it's realizing it's not worth making a meal out of mealtimes.

It's no big deal, if or how they eat their food. Its minimising mealtime anxiety that's most important.

RESISTANT EATERS

When children are anxious around mealtimes, their appetites are naturally suppressed. Their fight or flight response gears them up to fight off our attempts to force-feed them or fuels them up to run away. This causes their body to suppress hunger as it deals with a perceived threat, exacerbating the issue as they no longer feel hungry for anything, including those few foods they would normally eat. But don't fear, even if they skip a few meals, a fussy eater won't starve, despite their food choices being small and limited.

But cause for concern would be if a child was very selective over their food persistently and consistently, causing nutritional deficiencies. This can happen for reasons out of a child's control such as if they have a disability, for instance, autism. A resistant eater may go days, even weeks, without eating. Resistant eaters are rare and need professional help. They may have an underlying physical, mental, or emotional impairment, preventing them from eating or causing difficulties such as coordination, digestion, chewing, or swallowing.

If worried, it's a good idea to keep a daily food diary, recording what they are eating, when, and the quantity.

Find out:

- If their height and weight is normal. If unsure, ask your Health Visitor, School Nurse, or GP.
- All the foods they do like to eat, there's probably more than you think.
- How much they eat, when and what it is.
- If they have difficulty eating food such as chewing [most young children struggle with chewing meat].

- If they are fine at eating crisps, biscuits, sweets, or chocolate (this is usually a good sign all is well).
- Is there a certain pattern to the types of food they eat e.g. certain colour, taste, or texture?
- If they have developed a habit for only eating their favourite food.

A variety of different coloured fruits and vegetables are nutritionally better. And, not liking sprouts but loving broccoli is fine, just give them extra broccoli.

Regardless if carrots are hidden in a Spaghetti Bolognaise or visible in a Roast Dinner, all food ends up the same way once it has been eaten. If they prefer mash potato, then we can just mash their boiled potatoes up with a folk; it's still the same potato.

SWALLOWING OUR OWN ADVICE

When children develop a preference for certain foods, it's because they were allowed to. It's not their fault. They don't do the grocery shopping. We buy, prepare and cook the food. The only thing we don't do is eat it for them. Maybe we should?

If you're at the end of your tether with your fussy eater, you could try the following exercise;

Go shopping for all the foods you hate most and make yourself a generously sized meal out of them. Then for fun, get your child to feed you. Then you'll be able to experience what mealtimes can be like for them.

The best way to influence their eating habits is to eat healthily ourselves. When they see us enjoying a bowl of fruit, they're more likely to do the same. Sometimes, we allow our children to eat unhealthily and remain inactive when we feel guilty about our own bad habits. It's often easier allowing them to join us than it is for us to change. After all, we can't expect them to resist temptation when we struggle, so telling them to do what we can't causes conflict and confusion. The only option is to incorporate some physical activity together in Us Time and not to buy these foods. Most children will choose cake over carrots because they just don't understand the health benefits of choosing the carrot over cake, and of course, cake is sweeter, giving their brains a sugar rush. If we stack their plate with carrot sticks at a party, while others load theirs with cake, obviously, they'll get upset.

We have to allow everything in moderation, or they'll blame us for denying them rather than thank us for taking care of their health. These foods are not bad when they have a little of them now and again. The issue is, it's hard to moderate these types of foods. They are empty calories that don't fill them up but leave them wanting more and more. And they don't eat them to satiate themselves, snacking is more of a past time.

CONSCIOUS CONTROL

Over time, this can cause overeating, even if they're not hungry, they'll somehow always find room for sweets. Conscious control is what's needed. Children need to learn how to stop themselves eating for the sake of it, or else they'll stop recognizing that full feeling. We can help them to feel that signal of fullness in their belly again by getting them to eat and drink consciously. This means no watching TV, playing or walking around while eating. Instead, they should be sat at the table, identifying with the food they're eating.

Ask them to discuss each mouthful before it enters their mouth, e.g. 'I'm going to have a bite of my shiny, fat, brown, sausage'

Using these colourful, adjectives, keeps them focused on their food in a fun way, psychologically filling them up quicker too. Slowing down their eating speed, chewing more slowly, putting cutlery down on the table after each mouthful, and making sure they don't fill their utensils with food also helps. All of this allows time for their food to go down, letting them know when they are full.

SIZE MATTERS

Being conscious is not about eating less food, it's eating more of the right food to avoid unhealthy snacking.

Children need healthy, filling foods like hearty vegetable soups and stews with a high water and vegetable content. Portion sizes should be small enough not to overwhelm them, yet enough to satisfy, so they're not left feeling hungry, needing anything else to eat.

As loving parents, it's tempting to give more than less food on our children's plate so they're not hungry later on, but this doesn't work.

If they overeat at lunchtime, they will not eat less to compensate at dinner time, they actually end up eating more.

It's possible to offer a second helping later if still hungry, but not to take the food out of their stomach once full.

Hunger can be mistaken for thirst, so we're better off offering them a drink of water before offering more food.

If after eating their meal they're still hungry, offer fruit or vegetables, this way, they'll get their recommended five portions a day. If they refuse them, they aren't really hungry, just looking for a sugar or salt fix or emotional eating.

EMOTIONAL EATING

Food used to comfort, reward, or control children leads to emotional eating, resulting in excess weight.

If children think food is the answer, this can develop into a friend they turn to in times of stress, upset, boredom, loneliness, or when they feel deserving of a reward. Sweet treats are an unhealthy reinforcer for good behaviour, which quickly turns into a reinforcer for bad behaviour. Children see sweets as a good thing, so in their absence, they misbehave. When I'm good, I eat sweets, when I'm not, I don't eat sweets. So, when we try to discourage a sweet eating habit, we are actually encouraging them to misbehave.

If they hurt themselves and we offer them a biscuit to comfort them, which usually does the trick, we instill the habit of eating junk when they are feeling hurt or down, while allowing them to eat when bored makes food their hobby.

Problems need dealing with, not food.

Emotional eating becomes a habit that as adults they will turn to to reward themselves for achievement or to console their sadness. Food then symbolizes a friend.

There should be no punishment or reward for eating or not eating, it's not good if they eat everything, and it's not bad if they don't eat anything.

Nutritious meals like Fish or Cottage pie, Roast dinner, soups, and stews are the only type of comfort that should be provided by the food we offer our children.

We control our children's food environment, if we provide their food, they shouldn't need pocket money to buy additional snacks.

We have to be firm and take this issue seriously. If they are eating outside the home, we need to educate them on nutrition, enabling them to make good, independent food choices.

We can also help by:

- Increasing the vegetable portions in each meal.
- Providing fruit as a snack.
- Not buying junk food.
- Clearing out our kitchens of all unhealthy snacks and treats, particularly with sugar such as biscuits, cakes, chocolate, sweets, pop, fruit juice, and crisps.
- Using smaller plates and bulking food with beans, pulses, and vegetables—not trying to eat less, but healthier.
- Buying bottled water or providing water in their drink bottles for school.
- Swapping white carbohydrates such as bread, rice, and pasta for wholemeal varieties.
- Swapping sugary cereals for high fibre ones or low-fat yoghurts or wholemeal toast.

- Making sure they don't eat anything else for at least twenty minutes after eating as they may not realise they are full before then and will overeat. It takes around twenty minutes for food to travel through the intestine. If they're still hungry, then we can offer them something nutritious to eat.

We can't hide our children from all this food seduction, but we can educate them. Helping them to make more informed, healthier, food choices by making food fun, not fast.

FOOD FOR FUN

Just as we discovered in the previous chapter, exercise, we have to make it fun for our children to want to adopt a habit.

Food can be fun, and we have to show them how.

A small vegetable patch in the garden, window box, or allotment can be a great investment, providing fresh air, fruit, vegetables, nature, exercise, education, and a fun hobby for some Us Time together.

Involving them with food shopping, preparation, and spending time discussing ingredients and where they come from, looking at recipe books, watching cookery programmes, and the cooking and preparing of meals provides children with basic general knowledge and understanding of the world.

A lot of children today think their food originates from a Supermarket. We can educate them about food and where it comes from when we involve them and grow our own, this encourages healthier eating too. Sowing, planting, picking, preparing, and cooking their own food teaches them the whole food process, from where it comes from to how it ends up on their plate. And provides a sense of achievement and pride, helping them feel connected to the food they eat, as well as encouraging them to experiment with new foods they wouldn't normally.

Assisting us in meal preparation will also teach them mathematical concepts such as weighing, timing, and food in its natural state, and the scientific changes it goes through, such as solids melting.

Giving them a part to play at meal times by way of laying the table and helping us out also boosts their self-esteem. And having a regular mealtime routine ensures they get the right type of food they need at the right time.

MEALTIME ROUTINE

Children need regular meal times at the same time each day as their body gets naturally hungry around the times they usually eat.

Eating together as a family is a great way to spend some Us Time together, chatting about the day. But if you don't eat until late, it's best to let them eat alone rather than wait. Adults can go longer periods than children without food.

Children are more active and use their energy throughout the day, requiring food to refuel.

Eating late can mean they're too tired to eat or by the time their food has arrived, they're starving and either swallow it down in one go or take a long time to eat it.

They need enough time to enjoy and digest their food. Feeling rushed or going to bed on a full stomach is uncomfortable and can affect their sleep.

TABLE MANNERS

Everyone has different attitudes toward table manners determined by culture, tradition, upbringing, habits, and personal preferences. Too much emphasis on table manners though can negatively affect children's behaviour, resulting in them eating very little of what we want them to. Although it's civilized in the Western World to use a knife and fork, it wasn't always that way, and some cultures today still eat with their hands. It's quite natural for children to want to do this rather than using cold metal utensils. Touching, smelling, and exploring food enables them to learn about what they eat. Their little fingers and thumbs are full of hundreds of sensors, this is how they learn about textures, temperatures, taste, and consistency.

How food gets into their mouth isn't the main priority, enjoying food is.

Resisting our temptation to spoon feed them allows them to learn to feed themselves, they'll work out society's rules and adjust when the time is right.

In the comfort of our own home, we don't have to waste time and energy telling them off or insisting they eat with cutlery.

There need to be some rules though, as a matter of health and safety. Staying seated at the table to eat so they don't choke and practising basic manners such as 'please' and 'thank you' are important.

However, being too strict and insisting on too many rules, can be too much to remember or too difficult to stick to.

Eating out socially and observing others shows them appropriate etiquette.

Understandably, we may be reluctant to take them out to a restaurant if they misbehave or lack basic table manners. Yet practising is the only way they'll ever learn how to behave while eating out in public.

WAITER-MINUTE

We have to put ourselves in our children's shoes if we want to succeed at positively influencing them.

Many parents find food and mealtimes a constant battle. As we end this final part of the routine, I'd like you to imagine how you would feel if you went to a restaurant and the waiter chose a meal for you that you disliked, and then tried force feeding or blackmailing you into eating it? While at the same time insisting the order you ate the food in, such as vegetables first, keeping a running commentary throughout on how they wanted you to behave, such as no talking or dessert until you had completely finished your main course?

I'm sure we wouldn't want to go back there again in a hurry!

How our children feel is more important than making sure they eat their greens with a fork. If they forcefully manage to swallow a sprout but feel sad, sick and miserable in the process, then what's the point?

Instead, let's join in with the laughter as they pour a bowl of spaghetti over their head. Those are classic, memory making moments, and great photo opportunities to keep for the future.

Everything, including food, provides our children with opportunities to learn for themselves.

The Routines set out in this book are important in helping children learn healthy habits. But we have to always remember—it's not so much what we do as parents (we are learning too and won't always get it right), but what's important is why and how we do it, and how everyone feels in the process. We will explore learning and how to feel good about it next!

CHAPTER 10:
LEARNING FUN FOR EVERYONE

KNOWLEDGE IS POWER

KNOWLEDGE IS POWER. BUT power without purpose is pointless. The more children understand about the world they live in, the better life choices they will make. But it's all worthless and ineffective if they don't use what they learn in the real world. A head full of facts is simply mental clutter, anyone can memorize times tables and spellings. It's organizing that learning and putting it to test in everyday life that counts. For that, children need hands-on practice and common sense as much as knowledge. They don't need high IQ's or photographic memories or to be good at certain subjects such as Maths or English to learn. All they have to do is be interested, enthusiastic, and want to learn—then learning becomes inevitably naturally easier and more fun.

Our children want to learn, and they love nothing more than sharing what they have learnt with others, and this is the real power of knowledge. And once they've learnt something, they can't really unlearn it, if taught the sky is blue, they will always know that fact to be true. That learning is retained when they're learning about something that interests them. The beauty is, in Pre-school, they are constantly learning through play and don't even know they're learning. But when they start school, that learning becomes more important, and it has a purpose. Suddenly, they are measured against a standard and have expectations set that aren't their own, and that's when learning is often regarded as no longer fun!

UNDER PRESSURE; PUSH THEM TO SUCCEED OR PUSH THEM OVER THE EDGE?

Push our children to succeed or push them over the edge, it's a fine line to tread.

Knowing how far to push them and when is unique to each parent and child. It's something that intuitively and instinctively we come to know the more proactive and involved we become in their learning and behaviour. Knowing this releases a lot of the pressure, which is essential if we want our children to do well. When children feel pressure to get something right, win, or be the best, they end up dreading any kind of challenge.

We have to push our children sometimes, and of course, yes, they will have to learn stuff they don't want to, that they may never even need to know in the future, especially when they start school. Their lesson here is self-discipline and determination, and that's a good enough lesson in itself. However, there are many children who struggle with formal classroom learning and who appear to be misbehaving at school. Instead of experiencing excitement from fun activities and learning new things, they end up feeling fear and anxiety over the unknown.

In these cases, how the teachers and how we as parents approach their behaviour and learning is detrimental to how they continue to learn and behave. Approaches should be unique to the individual child, as not all children learn the same way.

STARTING SCHOOL

What a boring world it would be if we all liked doing the same things, the same way.

Without variety and differences, conversation would soon dry up.

Yet we still expect our children to endure subjects that just don't interest them.

One day, I hope the school curriculums will include more variety and options. Offering more choice for children, especially for those who aren't naturally academic, to enjoy their learning, doing things that inspire and motivate them.

A lot of current issues that are happening on our streets today concerning children and crime, I believe, are due to children not feeling unique and special as they are with the abilities they've been given. A lot of children just don't realise their true potential or hidden talents because they haven't been given the chance to discover them. And many children have self-limiting beliefs that go unchallenged, holding them back, making them feel overlooked or rejected by a school system that makes them feel less than what they really are. They are measuring their potential in life based on their current circumstances and academic ability, but these may not always be favourable for all. It can be hard to see past the present moment and the environment that surrounds them to envision a different more successful future.

Times have changed, especially over the past decade, and the way we teach and treat our children needs to change too. Children are rebelling over the school system because they are not happy. I'm all for rules and routines—they are essential—but we also have to respect children's views on how they want to learn and create boundaries within those. We have to be more creative in our approach and endeavour to make learning fun for everyone. Allowing for more sporting and artistic talents to be a part of the school curriculum, giving them equal emphasis and recognition as the more traditional core subjects.

I mean, who actually gets paid more, a footballer or a mathematician?

Not all children aspire to be in intellectual careers. Some want to enjoy what they do, using their hands and creativity, such as flower arranging or making fancy cupcakes. Life is about being happy and healthy, not unhappy and wealthy. So, money and future aspirations aside, lets focus more on the present and on how our children are experiencing life right now. Because how they feel right now will have a bigger impact on their future than any qualification or career aspiration. It's good to arrive and achieve big goals but they've got to feel good when they get there and realise when they have arrived too. All the qualifications in the world won't empower our children in the future and make them happy. In today's world, they aren't even a guarantee of job security either. Happiness is a state cultivated from a young age. We come to expect what we get and get what we expect as we grow older. Happy, optimistic children who follow their own dreams and enjoyment succeed and find rare opportunities that are otherwise hidden from those clutching at hard-earned grades, who settle for a safe job for the sake of money in fear of failure or lack. Some children just can't stand sitting in a classroom, memorising facts that are of no relevance to them. However, this doesn't mean they shouldn't be taught these subjects alongside the things they do enjoy learning.

We just have to get the balance right and find more interesting ways to make those subjects that they dislike more enjoyable. We can start fuelling their passion by encouraging them in those areas they do enjoy and are good at, and by finding each child's preferred learning method. Some children, understandably, prefer a more hands-on approach, rather than theory.

After all, life is about putting learning into practice. Little use knowing what to do but not knowing how to do it, is there?

Let's, explore the different learning methods available to our children then.

LEARNING MODALITIES

Every child will have a preferred way of learning, some prefer:
- Listening—this is called 'Auditory learning'.
- Watching—'Visual learners'.
- Others prefer a more, hands-on approach—'Kinaesthetic learning' also known as 'tactile learning' by doing.

Identifying their preferred method or modality will make learning more interesting and fun. And it can also prevent children becoming misunderstood. A child who is labelled naughty may have difficulty sitting still and listening to a story on the mat in nursery. But may enjoy a class assembly where they get to act out a story or watch someone else do so.

They may simply not be auditory learners but more visual or kinaesthetic, and this affects how they behave and learn.

To find out your child's modality, watch them playing and listen carefully to the questions they ask.

Do they want to know what something looks, sounds, or feels like?

Most children use all modalities but usually prefer one.

Encouraging them to experiment with different ways of doing things helps them to nurture their learning and creativity. Reading them a story at bedtime such as 'Picnic Time with Bear', then the next day getting them to dress-up and role play having a teddy bears picnic in the garden, followed by watching or listening to the cartoon, will cover all the learning options in a fun, engaging way that all children can learn from and relate to. This way, they are exploring the visual, kinaesthetic, and auditory options, and if the lesson within the 'Picnic Time with Bear" book was on the topic of healthy eating, and we organise a teddy bears picnic with lots of healthy food such as fruit and vegetables, then they will also experience smell and taste (gustatory modality). All together, these layer upon their learning, appealing in more ways than one.

CREATIVITY

The reason why our children's behaviour may be wrongly judged by others is because formal learning can be too rigid. It often relies on right or wrong answers or certain ways of doing things. It's usually logical, and children usually aren't. They are naturally creative and creativity is open to many different possibilities and outcomes.

There's always more than one way to learn, that's why there's no need limiting our children to 'the right way' thinking. When learning, allowing them to explore all the options and to choose one that feels right to them is best. Doing the same things in exactly the same way or the right way stifles and disallows creativity. Lessening the chances of our children trying out or learning new things in different ways, resulting in no new connections in their brain being made. By doing things differently to the norm, our children become more flexible and comfortable in new learning endeavours.

Offering opportunities to learn in new and exciting ways that aren't fixed with only 'right way' outcomes gives all children the chance to participate. While demonstrating that there's always more than one way to do something, we also encourage creativity. Children will love this fresh new approach to learning, so try giving the following a go just for fun. Try getting your child to put their pyjamas on to go to the park, or putting their uniform on to go to bed, or putting milk in the cereal bowl before the cereal, or read a book back to front.

This is not as illogical as it may seem. Not only will you enhance your child's creativity by encouraging them to approach something differently to the norm, but by changing well established methods of learning, you change your child's brain. This triggers new connections in their brain cells to fire, causing new ideas to develop. That's why it's a good idea to jig our children's thought process up occasionally. To illustrate this, imagine there were many ways out of a burning building. Wouldn't we all rather our children take the quickest, safest, easiest route out through the window rather than the right way through the fire and out through the front door?

But this relies on them being creative enough to realize that there are many other ways out. They can't be limited by only one or the right way thinking. They have to think fast of all the possible options available to them and take action despite it being different to the norm.

It's the same when it comes to learning. Creative imagination is more important than knowledge. Doing things differently causes new and different neural connections to be made in their brain, allowing for more creativity, thinking out of the box, and a more exciting, broader variety of experiences.

Would we prefer our children to memorize insignificant facts that someone else in history has created, or to create history?

Our children have access to so much knowledge with the internet today. Anything they are unsure of can be found within seconds if they learn how to read and use a computer. As long as they have these resources, then no information will be out of their grasp. They don't need to store endless data in their minds, cluttering up their thoughts and creativity. They just need to be able to find the answers when they need to.'

The reality is, however, when they start real school, some topics taught won't interest our children, leaving them bored, distracted, or left behind.

So, how can we convince and motivate our children that learning is fun in those circumstances or if they find certain subjects difficult?

First, we must let go of those tendencies where we encourage our children to compete and achieve. Instead, we should encourage them to enjoy the process of learning at their own pace. We are not talking about sporting pursuits here, where some healthy competition and achievement are essential, although even then, we should be cautious.

Pressure to perform and achieve is what causes children anxiety and what sucks all the ease, fun, and enjoyment out of learning something new. When children are having fun, it doesn't feel like learning, and If children have no obvious expectations imposed upon them, and nothing to lose or live up to, they become free from the burden of being perfect and relax. Relaxation is the key to creativity and clear focused thinking, which is why this 'nothing ventured, nothing gained' attitude helps the less-abled children to succeed and enjoy activities more than the abled ones, who worry that they have to achieve a certain outcome. Conscientious children usually have expectations imposed upon them, sometimes from other people such as parents and teachers, but mostly, they come to imprison themselves with their own high, sometimes unrealistic, expectations of themselves. Their self-talk is usually harsh and implies they should or must achieve the highest or best rather than being open to learning new things. They think they should automatically be good at new things, and so they set themselves up psychologically to fail. Few people are ever good at anything new to begin with, but the people who become great at what they do are ones who learn from mistakes, failures, and experience. They have the opportunity to learn a lesson from every angle, not just the right one, so they naturally become more knowledgeable on a subject. As well as conscientious children, there are some less abled children who do not know this, who view their mistakes as a reflection on their ability and self, believing they are no good at something and will never be any good at it when really, all any child really needs is what I call the 4 P's in the Pod!

Don't worry I'll share those sweet P's with you soon!

It's natural we want our children to do well at school, but if we become too involved and take over, we miss the point of what the learning objective is.

When children are set homework projects at school, the whole point of the exercise is for our children to learn something by doing it themselves. Hopefully while enjoying the process as much as they can. As well-meaning parents, sometimes it can be hard to let our children do this for themselves and easier for us to do it for them. Yes, maybe it does feel rewarding watching our children parading our elaborate creations on the school yard.

And naturally, seeing how proud our children feel doing so, makes us feel good.

But do we want our children to feel proud of our efforts or their own?

Teachers want to see what the children can create and what they've learnt in the process, not what we are capable of. Teachers also have a good understanding of our children's ability more than we do. They'll know that it's our work not our children's if we produce an artistic masterpiece or solve an almost unsolvable equation. Of course, we can make a cardboard dinosaur better than our five-year-old can, but where's the fun in that if they have to watch us?

They don't care how perfect it looks. It's getting messy and having fun in the process that counts. We can still help if our children are finding something challenging but stepping back at times may be a good idea, there's plenty of time, and our children's learning is a constant process. It doesn't start on their first day at school and end the minute they leave school. Each new thing they learn builds on the last and consolidating all of that learning takes time. We want our children to understand what they are learning so they can apply it in real life in the real world. Hoarding a headful of useless facts won't help them in a real job. Bearing this longer-term goal in mind helps us relax. Knowing there's no race for our children to get any learning over and done with.

Ultimately, why do we want our children to learn something?

Why do we want them to do well and succeed?

The answer is to be happy, therefore, happiness is the ultimate goal and is the feeling we need to focus on our children experiencing.

Our children have to have a why.

Why do I need to know this?

The answer to that question becomes their motive, which is vital because the key to motivation in life is having a motive.

Why? What? Where? When? And How? All are incessant questions of our young. If we can just keep answering these, they will be constantly learning something new every day! Having fun in the process makes things easier for us and more enjoyable for our children, so try playing games as opposed to lecturing or just reeling off answers.

THE END RESULT GAME

One game children enjoy playing is 'The End Result Game.' We touched on this in Food for Fun in the previous chapter when we mentioned involving our children in growing their own food. Sowing, planting, picking, preparing, and cooking their own food teaches them the whole food process, from where it comes from to how it ends up on their plate.

We can also encourage their creative imagination by asking them to choose an object from their bedroom, then getting them to research the steps it took to create that thing, from end result to start. For example, when my son chose a book, we traced the steps backward from purchasing it from the internet, getting it delivered by courier to it coming from a publisher, who printed and bound and commissioned it, to the ideas coming from the author's imagination, and the illustrations coming from the artist, to the paper coming from the tree etc. This game gives children the chance to see the collaboration that takes place between people and places and the use of imagination to bring them all together for a simple book.

What we don't want to be is an obvious teacher, we can enrich our children in many ways, but hothousing is a 'no, no' in my book when it comes to happy, healthy, and successful children.

DON'T BE AN OBVIOUS TEACHER

All children enjoy the time and attention that listening to a story or doing a puzzle brings. They want to learn, but we don't want them to feel like they are learning, we want them to feel like they're having fun. If they are disinterested in learning activities, we need to ask ourselves the following questions:

- Is this appropriate for my child's age or stage of development or am I reading such a simple book, my five-year-old could read it to them-self?
- Is the content/activity interesting?
- Am I engaging my child enough?
- Am I actually interested myself, or am I bored and disinterested?
- Do they think there's a purpose to the activity other than having fun or spending time together?
- Have I taken them away from another activity or toy that they were enjoying playing with?

The biggest influence that we can have is our own enthusiasm and interest. When we are engaged, characters and learning come to life and stimulate them more. Conventional learning styles such as story time on the mat at school or learning their times tables bores them rigid. If we want our children to concentrate on learning, we need to find things they enjoy playing with. If they can play for long periods with cars, then we can use those to play counting games. It's about us being creative and using our imagination as much as getting them to use theirs.

Every child learns at their own pace. Therefore, there's no point comparing our children's level of learning with anyone else's.

Just make learning fun, and give them a big enough motive and a bit of a challenge!

A BIT OF A CHALLENGE

As parents, watching our children struggle and fail is difficult. And as grown- ups, watching them can also be frustrating. As the old saying goes 'It's as easy as riding a bike.' Which suggests riding a bike is easy? But is riding a bike for the first time really easy?

It's easy to forget how hard something is to do when we can already do it!

If we want to help our children, we have to keep in mind that everything is hard to them until they learn how to do it. Another word for parent is patience! Where do you think our children learn patience from?

Yes, from us, their parents, that's why modelling patience toward our children is vital, as an impatient child is seen as misbehaving, rarely as eager. Any new endeavour our children attempt will be challenging. And like everything else, it becomes easy when they know how.

Part of the fun of learning something is the challenge it brings and the sense of achievement that our children feel when they've mastered something new.

That's why, without challenge, their brains and bodies cannot be stretched and they cannot learn anything new or gain self-confidence in themselves through achievement.

It's not just the act of learning something in itself, like the skill of riding a bike that our children have to contend with, but before they can brave it alone and start practising, there's other necessary components such as feeling safe, relaxed, and confident that also need to be addressed. That's why they may interpret any challenge, such as learning to ride a bicycle, as too scary, hard, boring, time consuming, impossible, or even as a punishment. Particularly, if we expect them to get it right straight away or we become irritated and impatient with their progress. Under these circumstances, learning is no fun. And when they feel forced to do something they are afraid of or anxious about, they react with unwanted behaviour, i.e. a tantrum!

We know we are only trying to help, so it's easy to become annoyed with them and add fuel to their already raging fire. Teaching them how to ride a bike is not only a useful skill, but once they've mastered it, they'll have lots of fun. We know that, so that's the message we somehow have to positively convey to our children, despite their tears and tantrums.

STEP BY STEP

To do that, firstly, we must show them that whatever they are trying to learn is possible.

Let's take the riding a bike example. By explaining that we too could not ride a bike once and how we fell off many times—face planted on the floor—until we learnt and practised often, reassures them it's okay to fall off and fail. But more importantly, that in the end, it's still possible to master with practice, and it's because of falling off and hurting themselves that they will learn to stay on the bike, not in spite of it. Then their motivation becomes not falling off their bike and getting hurt to begin with. The next step is to show them how to ride a bike, step by step.

Gradually building their self-confidence up by allowing them to practice using stabilizers, then by us holding onto them when the stabilizers first come off, until they feel ready to go it alone.

The trick is always keeping them focused mentally as well as physically in the direction they want to go in. And most importantly, by making it a fun learning experience, that they'll want to repeat and will look forward to doing.

This way, they'll find any new learning challenge as easy as riding a bike!

If they find something too easy, we can be sure they are not learning anything new or making any new neural connections in the brain.

We don't want to overwhelm them though or set impossible challenges. It's better to increase their confidence step by step by:

- Revising what they are already good at.
- Developing and improving on what they are already good at or what they already know.
- Stretching their abilities bit by bit.
- Gradually increasing and introducing new learning challenges.
- Steering their learning at their own pace

Any learning experience can be daunting in its entirety. But if taken step by step, little by little, by putting all those steps together, any task becomes manageable and eventually complete. If our children are faced with a problem or feeling overwhelmed by homework, teaching them to break it down into stages and dealing with it bit by bit will make it less daunting. As well as easier and quicker to solve.

Using this method, children learn that they can do anything, no matter how difficult it initially seems. All we have to do is be there for them, supporting, encouraging, and loving them for all their efforts, not just their achievements. As long as progress is being made, so will mistakes. A child who is learning to use the toilet independently will still get dirty pants from time to time. That is learning in progress. There's no need to be afraid of our children developing slowly, any development is progress. We just need to be concerned if they're not developing at all. If children feel under pressure to perform, they can easily or suddenly regress or shut down. Being patient while learning will encourage them to persist and succeed. Learning a new skill presents a lot more than they realise, they learn how to persevere, build self-confidence, and that nothing is impossible or too difficult with a little 'Positivity, Practice, Patience, and Persistence. We call these the four P'S in a Pod.

THE 4 P'S IN A POD – POSITIVITY, PRACTICE, PATIENCE, & PERSISTENCE

It's important our children know that practise is key to acquiring new skills and learning, not just their ability, socioeconomic background, or luck.

They need to understand that it's those who keep trying who are the most successful in their endeavours, not just the gifted or fortunate.

Whether it's learning to tie their shoe laces or becoming a world class chess champion, in any endeavour, no matter how difficult a task may seem, following the four P's creates results.

These are:
1. Positivity
2. Practice
3. Patience
4. Persistence

When it comes to learning anything, these are like four magic peas in a pod. When these four combine, there's no such thing as failure, and success is just part and parcel of the process.

We need to encourage our children to keep at whatever they are learning, no matter how difficult it may appear at first. Once they see that eventually they do learn and can do the things that once they could not do, this motivates them in future endeavours.

We can back this up with past experiences. For example, if they are struggling to learn a new topic in school, we can remind them of a time when once they could not ride a bike or swim, and how it took time, Positivity Practice, Patience, and Persistence.

This should keep them trying, even when things don't appear to be going right. As parents, we also need to follow these four P'S when helping or teaching our children too.

POSITIVITY

Any negative thoughts or feelings on the subject they wish to learn will only hold them back in their progress. Especially if they think they are no good at something or believe they will never be able to learn it.

Negativity sets our children up to fail. It scuppers motivation, dampens enthusiasm, clouds intention, and takes all the fun out of learning something new and exciting.

Nothing seems possible without a certain degree of positivity. Which is why a positive outlook to learning is vital to success. When learning, any challenges or uncertainty along the way should be embraced as a positive. This is what highlights the areas that need attention and the very beginning of progress, not failure. Children shouldn't feel like they must catch up with everyone else, they should decide the pressure they're going to experience. By setting their own learning goals and expectations, they can positively affect their achievement by thinking and feeling good about it, as opposed to thinking or feeling negatively.

By encouraging our children to give themselves a pat on the back for their accomplishments whenever they learn something new, they'll learn to be their own mentor and best friend. Then, when we are not around to cheer them on and keep them positive, they can do so for themselves.

But when we can, every effort as well as accomplishment, big or small, is worthy of our reward and praise. It fuels our children's motivation to achieve more and more. Not for the reward themselves, but for the recognition they bring. I see very clever, conscientious children succeed at everything they do, and after a while, they receive no praise, reward, or recognition. It's as if it's just what is expected of them. Anything less than the best is not enough. These children work hard for the sake of pleasing others and keeping their reputation, but they deserve to be acknowledged for each individual thing they achieve, no matter how small—no achievement should be taken for granted.

Rewards need not be grand or expensive, simply a trip to the park or a 'well done' is enough for most children. Simple gestures or acknowledgements can make learning a positive, worthwhile experience for all children.

Luckily, most young children naturally display a sunny disposition. They like to think of the best outcomes, often saying things how they would like them to be. However, even the most positive child will encounter difficulties when learning something new.

Affirmations are a great aid in lifting up moods and creating confidence in our children. We have already looked at these in chapter 7— Esteem, but here's a few more to refresh. Whenever they encounter difficulties, we can try and encourage them to repeat to themselves these positive, affirming, statements:

'I can do it!'

'Anything is possible.'

'Every day in every way, I am learning more and more.'

They will be able to learn anything they desire, regardless of their ability, if:

- We believe in them.
- They believe they can.
- They follow the four P'S. Patience, Practise, Persistence, and Positivity.

PRACTICE

They will get there in the end with practice, no matter how difficult something is. It's easy to drive to the shop if you have been driving for years, but it won't be easy if you have never driven a car in your life before. We need to understand this before we try to help our children to learn anything new.

Sounds obvious, yet, so many of us parents get frustrated easily when teaching our children, particularly when we've already taught them how to do something and they get it wrong.

But if we are going to be the vehicle through which our children learn, we need to make sure that we're learner friendly and that we can manoeuvre them in the right direction at the right time.

Take the driving example above, even if you have driven a car many times, you are still learning. There's so much to learn about driving, not just how to physically operate the car, but the green cross code, road signs, how to refuel and change oil or tyres etc.

It takes practice, time, and experience before you really feel confident as a driver. This analogy is good to remember when helping our children to learn. Let's say they're learning how to read. Just because they could read the word 'dog' yesterday, doesn't mean they'll remember it automatically today. They may still get confused and call it 'bog' the next day, d and b are the same as learning anything else, they take time, and are easy to mix up and confuse.

We think it's easy because we can read already, and have more than likely read daily for many years, which adds up to a lot of reading practice.

Reading is still new to our children though. It's like us learning a second language such as German, and someone expecting us to know and recognize words straight away. Then whenever we forget or get a word wrong, they get annoyed with us. I doubt we would still feel encouraged to carry on learning the language then?

Nothing is easy for our children, unless they can do it, in which case, they wouldn't need our help in the first place.

Try doing something you have never learnt to do before, such as knitting, skiing, or learning a new language.

Then see how difficult it is to begin with.

Observe how you learn to do it best.

Is it when you are rushed, angry, or frustrated with yourself?

Or when you have time, patience, practice, and are feeling relaxed, positive, and persistent?

When our children are practising something new, they will feel like they are getting it all wrong and they will be wondering if they will ever succeed.

Even though we know, eventually, they will, they won't always know this, we have to instil in them some patience.

PATIENCE BRINGS GOOD LUCK

One day, when my daughter was younger, she was having a particularly successful day. Not only had she received a Certificate and a sticker for being Star Pupil of the Week at school, (meaning she had the privilege of bringing the Class Teddy home for the weekend) but she also won some stationary in the School Prize Draw. Later that afternoon, she then went on to receive her next level Gymnastics Badge and Certificate at the Leisure Centre.

All in all, she was having a really good, successful day!

Then on the way home from Gymnastics she said to me:

'Mum, I was losing at everything and not doing so well for a couple of weeks, but now I'm doing good at everything, all in one day!'

I explained to her, that it did indeed seem to be happening all in one day, but really, when she felt as though she was not doing so well and 'Losing at everything,' she was in fact, doing better than she thought.

Taking those necessary steps on all those days leading up to that day and not giving up, even when it looked like she was losing, had led her to successfully winning so much in one day through her practice, patience, and persistence.

If she had lost her patience and quit Gymnastics when she wasn't doing so good, or gave up trying so hard at School when she felt like she was losing, then she would never have succeeded in getting better. Understanding the concept of the four P's and how they had worked for her, helped her to realise that even though it may look like she is not doing well at times or doing really well at others, it's all in fact a result of her succeeding. It was clear for her to see that it was her patience, practise, persistence, and positivity in the past that had created her successful day, not just a lucky day!

When our children realise how important patience is in succeeding to learn, they will be more likely to persist in their learning endeavours.

PERSISTENCE

Persistence is key to learning success. Even if at times they don't feel positive and they haven't practiced something in a while and they are feeling inpatient with themselves, if in the face of all that, they continue to persist, they will reach their goal in the end. That's why, if at first, our children don't succeed, we must encourage them to try, try and try again until they do!

They won't want to persevere if they don't want to learn something or feel they can't.

Overcoming this 'I can't' can be challenging in itself, but if we try, then our children will too.

I'm not fond of the word 'try' as it implies failure, but in our house, we have a saying to overcome the 'I cant's':

'I can't' is just 'I can' with a T for Try!'

This encourages reluctant children to try and overcome things they thought they couldn't.

Intelligence aside, when our children have a job in the grownup world, they will be expected to take action and make independent decisions without being told, taught, or shown. This takes common sense and initiative, both of which cannot easily be taught later on in life. It's developed by fostering independence early on, and providing our children with opportunities for them to try and learn for themselves.

LEARNING TO BE INDEPENDENT

As parents, we can help foster independence in our children, but, ultimately, being independent is something our children have to learn for themselves. That's why it's important that we do give them plenty of opportunities to gain independence

They can practice by putting their coats on, tying their shoelaces, wiping up spills, putting toys away, doing their homework, and saving their pocket money. Why do we do things for them that we know they are capable of doing themselves?

If we do everything for our children, we rob them of their independence. It's easier to do things for them that they should be able to do themselves when we are busy or stressed, usually out of frustration or because we are in a hurry. But they learn nothing from that. If they genuinely cannot do something themselves, then we can help while showing them what to do, otherwise, letting them do it for themselves is best.

Then, with enough patience and practice, they will be able to do it for themselves, but we shouldn't prevent them from trying or learning. This is when conflict arises. Children are normally fiercely independent, they want to do it themselves. If we try to prevent them doing something, they will do all they can to do it! Which is exactly what we want to teach them anyway... remember the 'I can do it' attitude?

Stepping back and allowing them is imperative because there's going to be things our children need to learn for themselves that we will never be able to teach them. Encouraging independence early on is crucial in teaching them how to cope in life. We can't spare them a broken heart when they get dumped, or deal with the rejection of not being picked for school prefect. And we won't be there to wipe their nose, take their exams, or fight their battles at school, they need to learn how to deal with those difficulties themselves. It requires a 'Can do!' attitude and persistence, especially when things get challenging.

Regardless of academic intelligence with this can-do attitude, children can learn anything by applying the Four P'S.

That's the theory anyway, so let's test it by doing a little experiment.

THE 4 P'S EXPERIMENT

Think of something your child would like to achieve or improve on.

It could be a subject in school or hobby such as flying a kite.

Choose only one thing or aspect and encourage them to use the four P's in achieving their goal (don't forget to also follow the four P's yourself when helping your child too!).

In the beginning, they may not find it easy. But with positive expectation, practice, and patiently learning what they need to, persisting when they make mistakes or things get difficult, they will eventually improve or achieve their learning goal.

Then you can use that as an example to motivate them and help them achieve any future goals.

Once they start seeing their successes and how the four P's have helped them to achieve what they have, be it a good grade at school or a new belt in karate, this will build confidence in their learning ability and will encourage them to keep trying new things and not to quit when things get tough.

Then the Four P'S will become a habit they adopt and use automatically for everything they do in their life.

All our children need to do is positively practice, patiently and persistently, embracing the challenge. And that, along with the seven steps to success in our final chapter presented next, will create unlimited success!

CHAPTER 11:
THE SEVEN STEPS TO SUCCESS

WHAT IS SUCCESS?

OUR CHILDREN'S HAPPINESS IS the true measure of both our parenting success and that of our children's success, not their achievements. Other than happiness, any other accomplishments they achieve are just added bonuses. All that matters are that they're happy and working toward improving on their own personal best. Success is a very personal thing, meaning something different to each child. One child may feel they've succeeded by getting six out of ten in their spelling test, while another who got six out of ten may feel like a failure, especially if they were expecting or were expected by others to get ten out of ten. Children seldom measure themselves on their success, but on other people's expectations, meaning eight out of ten is good, unless a parent or teacher expects more. We make them feel successful by being happy with them for their efforts, as much as achievements. Children are naturally happiest when learning and achieving new things, but each child will have their own unique talents. These can sometimes be unrecognised as society, and the school system tends to associate talent with academic ability, often overlooking hidden talents in lesser known areas.

CELEBRATING SUCCESS

We can give our children the recognition they need by celebrating every success, big or small. The more children see their accomplishments, the more motivated they will be to build upon them. Success breeds success, but they have to believe in their ability to succeed. If they struggle at school, it can be difficult for them to believe in themselves, this is when it's more important than ever to celebrate their successes and spur them on. Our support is what will count toward the overall success they achieve in any endeavour. Whether that be financial support, such as paying for lessons, books, or equipment, or moral support by going along to their training practices or shows, or helping with homework and accepting their aspirations.

Our children's only goal is to be happy and have fun. Rarely do they long for success, that's usually our desire for them. All they want is to make us proud and to feel a sense of belonging, acceptance, and recognition. This is easily done by talking proudly about their achievements to others in front of them and displaying their success around the home, perhaps through framing their sporting or school certificates for the wall or making shelves to house their medals or trophies, and putting their certificates and paintings on the fridge for all to see.

It's also a good idea to keep a record of all of their personal attainments that they can build on throughout the years. This can be done in many ways, such as creating a folder for each child labelled Record of Achievements file or compiling scrapbooks to store letters, school reports, certificates, and badges, etc. These all keep them motivated to carry on achieving, as well as being good keepsakes to look back on when they are older.

Also, keeping photo albums, DVDS, or hanging photos of them around the home with family members and friends enjoying special occasions together, such as holidays or celebrations, instils their sense of belonging and unity in the world. Constantly reminding them of good times and experiences they have had, as well as all the people who care and love them. This helps to keep memories alive, as well as improving our children's recollection of events in their life. Without physical evidence, these memories soon fade, try asking your teenager about the first time they went swimming or their first holiday when they were younger and they will probably say they can't really remember it, unless of course it's a prominent photo they have looked at over the years.

Regardless of where their talents lie, if our children learn the 'Seven Steps to Success' outlined in this chapter, rest assured, they will be able to find the people and resources they need to unearth their talents and succeed, and along with the 4 P's, these will keep them on track to success.

KEEPING THEM ON TRACK

Most children know what they like and what motivates them, which is vital to staying enthusiastic and motivated. We just need to help them arrange their lives and keep them focused on their chosen goals when immaturity leads them astray. Children are fickle and their concentration spans short. Boredom soon sets in once the novelty has worn off any endeavour, making it easy for them to lose sight of the bigger picture of what they initially set out to achieve. It's so easy to view an obstacle or setback as an excuse to give up and quit. What we must do is prove to our children that these are just opportunities to grow and adapt through adversity in order to achieve an even better version of their original goal. We can help keep them on track to success by providing them with the right support, resources, experiences, equipment, education, and opportunities, and by being available and encouraging them in their endeavours. Whether they are learning how to read, ride a bike, or even origami, we need to acknowledge each step that they take along the way, instead of concentrating on the outcome of the goal itself. Then, by following The Seven Steps to Success outlined below, they cannot fail to succeed.

THE SEVEN STEPS TO SUCCESS

1. Enthusiasm
2. Aspiration
3. Intention
4. Motivation

5. Decisiveness
6. Failure
7. Resilience

These Seven Factors do not require our children to have a high IQ, academic genius, or natural giftedness. Just a keen willingness and an open receptive mind, along with us as their cheering squad. This keen willingness is enthusiasm, which is the first step toward success, often displayed as excitement.

ENTHUSIASM

The more excited children are about a thing, the better, because to succeed, they need to feel enthused. In any new endeavour, initially, they will naturally possess both enthusiasm and motivation, but over time, alongside setbacks, it can easily dwindle. Encouraging their enthusiasm is not always easy, especially if they are annoyingly excitable or if we feel their enthusiasm for something is misplaced. Sometimes, their aspirations and goals can seem extreme or far- fetched, or not in line with our own aspirations for them. However, we should avoid at all costs being the fire extinguisher that dampens or puts out our children's dreams and desires. We need to try to believe in them no matter how extreme, bizarre, farfetched, or below their potential they seem. Letting our children discover for themselves whether they are capable of succeeding in an endeavour through use of the Seven Steps fans the flames of their enthusiasm and helps them to ignite the fire in their belly. This fire, known as enthusiasm, comes from the word 'En Theos' in Greek, translated into English means 'Is God', so when our children are feeling enthusiastic, they are feeling their god within. Enthusiasm is powerful, it's what propels our children forward on the runway to success and gives flight to dreams and ambitions that otherwise would lay dormant and grounded. Enthusiasm will give them the power, motivation, and energy to be, do, or have anything they think they can, or in some cases, even things they think they can't can be achieved with enthusiasm. Children are naturally enthusiastic. As long as they stay that way, they are already on the road to success. We can keep their enthusiasm alive by offering plenty of new opportunities or things to challenge them and through planning special occasions they can look forward to. Even unpleasant experiences can be turned into something to feel enthusiastic over.

Once, my daughter was very enthusiastic about going into hospital and having an operation on her ears. She was counting down the days and even going to bed early in the evenings to make the time go quicker. She was excited to meet all the doctors and nurses, as she aspired to be one. She was also looking forward to her family and friends visiting her with treats and having a few days off school with both her parents. She was equally enthusiastic over her recovery, as she was looking forward to being able to hear properly again after surgery and going to the Cinema. There were only positive outcomes for my daughter, and this certainly helped her in her recovery after the operation. Whilst all the other children were upset, the nurses had to hold my daughter down to stop her getting up out of bed, as she was eager to get going again, even though the anaesthetic had not worn off. By painting a positive picture of events to our children no matter what the circumstances, and providing them with things to look forward to before, during, and after an event, they learn to see past the challenges and become enthusiastic to get on with things. We can apply this method to anything that we want our children to feel enthusiastic over, whether visiting Granny or learning how to swim. We can encourage their enthusiasm, but true enthusiasm comes from within them naturally. By allowing their passions and helping them to discover, realise, and achieve their own goals, dreams, and desires, we feed their enthusiasm. This is how they will achieve success. It's a good idea to know what our children are enthusiastic about. Their interests, and the people or places that make them feel excited, could be a sign of their future aspirations in life.

ASPIRATIONS

Aspiration is the next step to success; it's taking their desire for something they enjoy doing seriously enough to believe they can achieve future success in it. This gives them a goal to aim for, and with enough support and faith, they can realise their ambition. They could be enthusiastic about playing football in the park with friends, giving them the desire to go to football training with a Coach and join a club, playing for their local team, which could lead onto them playing Premiere League when they are good or old enough to do so. Their enthusiasm for the game becomes an aspiration with an objective in their life. They may not be good at school academically, but if football is their passion, then they have the chance to do something they love as a career, making them a lot of money whilst having fun and keeping fit at the same time. Some academically gifted, conscientious students are clueless what they want to do or become at the end of all their studying. Often, the lessons that they learn, Courses or Degrees, bear no relevance to the careers they eventually end up choosing. Allowing our children to follow their passions and go with what makes them feel enthusiastic in life, and to aspire to be who they want to be, is the real secret to success. The more they are encouraged to feel enthusiastic over their aspirations, the more they will learn how to do a thing because they enjoy it, instead of because they feel that they have to. Of course, not all wannabe footballers make it to the Premiere League, but that's not the point, even if they are not good enough to do so, they can still fulfil their aspirations by becoming a Football Coach or Sports Teacher. It's about aspiring to do something they love and choosing what will make them happy. However, it's worth noting that some aspiring young footballers do go onto Premiere League. Children can't be successful if they don't know what they are trying to succeed at, so goals and aspirations are essential to success, as long as it's their own aspirations and no one else's. In the absence of other people's opinions and limiting beliefs, children can realise their dreams. If we felt when we were younger becoming Prime Minister wasn't an aspiration that we could achieve, that doesn't mean our children can't. I suspect Margaret

Thatcher's parents didn't expect her to become the first female Prime Minister of the United Kingdom and the first female elected Head of National Government in Europe, but she did it!

From humble beginnings, we all grow, yet aspirations are not about deciding on a future career and sticking to it for the rest of their life though. What child could possibly know what one job to choose when they haven't even experienced working fulltime before?

Then, even when they realise their aspirations, once those aspirations become a fulltime job, all of the fun could disappear.

They may love playing football for leisure but find that as a job day in day out, it doesn't fulfil their every need. Conversely, if they obtain a Law degree but love baking cakes, then they're better off opening a cake shop instead. Success is not about ability or lack of it, it's about our children discovering what they want and happily doing it. As parents, we try to steer our children toward a safe, steady, lucrative career, but is money or working hard really what we want for our children, or would we prefer they do something that they love and that makes them happy?

HAIRDRESSER OR DOCTOR?

It's working happier not harder. Chances are, they will be healthier too if they enjoy what they do, and happy and healthy means they're more inclined to succeed in life and do well. There are no safe, steady, careers anymore, and hard graft and struggle makes no one happy or healthy, no matter how much they earn or how much status they think they have. I once heard a Mum scoff at her daughter's idea of becoming a hairdresser. 'Don't waste your life cutting other people's hair' she said, 'Get a Degree and become a Doctor or something that is going to make you some money.' I commented to that Mum that my hairdresser charged me one hundred and twenty-pounds last time I visited, and that's not bad for two hours' work doing something they enjoy. I suspect some doctors earn less for two hours' work.

Children's aspirations will change often over time, one day they may want to be a Fire Fighter, and another they may want to be a Pop Star, that's part of the fun of creating their own future. It's exciting knowing that they have the whole world before them to be and do anything they choose, limited only by their imaginations. How can any child know for certain what they want to be when they are older?

Even with knowledge and experience, preferences change in life, so why should they stick at one thing when there's so much out there to try?

If we want our children to become something specific, such as a Doctor, then maybe that's an aspiration we need to realise for ourselves.

Maybe we could retrain—it's never too late. The only aspirations we should have for our children is to encourage them to—in the words of Mark Twain: 'Make their vocation their vacation'.

INTENTION

Our children may be fuelled with enthusiasm for an aspiration, but what is their intention behind that aspiration?

We are in a better position to guide our children when we understand their intentions. When little, my son aspired like most young boys to be a Superhero. He had watched the cartoons, read the comics, and role played with the action figures. Dressing up in Superhero costumes long enough, he felt he knew all there was to know about being a Superhero, and he had the aspiration and enthusiasm to be that hero and do good in the world. To have discouraged my son would have been to shatter his dreams and aspirations into moon dust. I had to try and help him realistically keep his aspirations alive by finding out the essence of his intention, i.e. why he wanted to be a superhero?

Once I realised that he wanted to become a superhero to help and save people, I adapted the role to suit the situation. I explained in a way that he could understand for his age that people such as doctors, policemen, and firefighters are superheroes in disguise who help to save and protect people. He then went from wanting to be a superhero, to wanting to be a policeman who 'locked up all the baddies'. Understanding intention is the secret ingredient to success. If our children know why they want something, this helps them to know what they want, and this gives them a purpose. This sense of direction and clarity means they will be more likely to achieve the focus of their intention and to direct their moment by moment experiences. Asking them about their intentions in all areas of their life keeps them focused.

We might ask them what their intentions are when they next go to their gymnastics class.

They may say, 'I intend to see all my friends that I haven't seen since last week.'

Then we must be careful not to replace their intentions with our own by saying, 'Your intention should be to practice your spring boarding so you can aim for your next badge.' That would be our intention for them, not theirs. Meeting up with friends at gymnastics is a good intention in itself. When they have a reason to look forward to going, they'll feel motivated to go each week and naturally achieve their next badge in their own time. Our main intention is their happiness, and that's their intention for themselves too. Talking specifically about their intentions for the day ahead will give them clearer direction throughout the day too, even if it is just to be on time for school or to get along with friends. It's about planning ahead, but it doesn't matter if they don't achieve what they intend to, not every day turns out the way we plan it. The aim is for them to get into the habit of intending what they want to happen in their life. Then other people, situations, or their own emotions won't dictate to them as they choose the direction they go in. It's easy for our children to become influenced by those around them without daily intention. If their intention is to get along with friends at school and they find themselves in a dispute with friends, then instead of retaliating and being swept along with their friend's moods, they can remember their intention and decide to end the dispute amicably. That's the intention anyway, it may not always override their emotions, but it can keep them focused so that disruptions or challenges do not throw them off course easily. It also helps them to recognize when they have achieved whatever it is they have set out to achieve and keeps them motivated to take the necessary steps needed along the way to achieving their goal. If it's their intention to get their spellings right at school, they will be more likely to practise them. Their intention gives them a motive, and it's motive that is key to motivation.

MOTIVATION

Intention will motivate them to carry on when things don't work out the way they wanted or go to plan. According to Abraham Maslow [1954] *A Dynamic Theory of Human Motivation*; 'Our child's ultimate aim is to gain the motivation to develop their full potential in life, and once this has been achieved, they will find true happiness.

MY CHILD'S MOTIVATORS

Unfortunately, motivation doesn't last; it can disappear as quickly as it came. We have to encourage our children to keep moving forward. When we find out what motivates our children, we can use this to keep them motivated. Whether it's managing behaviour or helping them to learn, using what uniquely motivates them will lead to the greatest success.

Based on observations and active listening, you can learn more on how to do this in my book The Powerful Proactive Parent's Guide to Present Parenting, we can compile a short list of the things they like and dislike. Below is an example.

Likes and Dislikes List

1. Dislikes going to bed early.
2. Likes Swimming
3. Dislikes doing art and crafts

4. Likes doing puzzles.
5. Dislikes tidying bedroom.
6. Likes playing at the park.

It's important to include dislikes as much as like's because some children are more motivated by a consequence that they don't want to happen, such as going to bed earlier or having their favourite toy confiscated, than a reward such as a trip to the park. The first year that I wrote this list for my own children, I found it useful to refer to it whilst buying Christmas presents for them and ended up buying exactly the right presents. It can also give us ideas on what to do with our Us Time together, and ways in which we can motivate good behaviour. We just have to discover if our children are motivated by reward or by not losing something that they already have, such as not being allowed to play on their computer if they do not behave as opposed to gaining a sticker when they do behave. Below is a list of popular motivators with space for your own ideas:

- Sticker Charts
- Certificates
- Praise and Recognition
- Playing outside with friends on their bike/scooter/skates
- Visiting family and friends
- Going Swimming/Karate/Drama club/Fishing etc.
- Playing on their gaming devices, electronics
- Going to Cinema/Shopping
- Watching their favourite TV programme
- Walking the dog

Your list:

-
-
-
-
-

The list is not intended to blackmail our children, but simply to motivate them when enthusiasm wanes—although, undeniably, it can be a great negotiation tool. Letting them know that if they don't tidy up their toys, their friend won't be allowed over to play motivates them to tidy up. It's their toys and it's their friend they want to visit, therefore, they are doing it to benefit themselves. This art of negotiation is a method of communication that our children can understand, and it's a skill they will become good at. Children are master negotiators when they want something, so it's an area we need to practice in, and if it benefits them, then of course they will want to do it!

THE SECRET TO MOTIVATION IS A MOTIVE

Given a good enough reason, our children will be motivated, especially to do those things that they like. Sometimes, they may need a little convincing and a reason why they should before they do it.

Saying 'That's why' won't motivate them, we need to be a little more proactive in our approach. Maybe the incentive of a new comic if they help with the chores will? Knowing what motivates them, will make all of the difference to the outcome. If, for instance, we want them to get ready for their swimming lesson, but they are absorbed in another activity, demanding they do it because we say so will not motivate them, especially if they are enjoying what they are already doing. But if we re-phrase it by explaining that after swimming they can then carry on doing what they enjoy uninterrupted, with the added bonus of a swimming certificate for passing their level in swimming that they can add to their file and show grandma on the way home, they will see the benefits and hopefully take decisive action to get changed and go to their swimming lesson.

DECISIVNESS

Over time, this method will help them to become self-motivated, making independent decisions for themselves. Instead of procrastinating and putting off their homework until later, they will come to understand the benefits of doing it straight away so they can relax. Making decisions is part of growing up, and it's an important life skill our children will need to learn. Strangely enough, nearly all children start out in life being very decisive, they know exactly what they want and when. Somehow, they lose this ability and become swayed by others, doubtful of themselves as they deliberate whether something might work out better another way. They learn to reason more and worry about what others think, causing their own innate ability to know and decide for themselves to get lost in a fog of confusion. Then, instead of being enthusiastic and going with their own feelings, they become paralysed by fear, wondering what someone else's decision would be. Even making small choices such as what dessert they would like can turn into a major decision as they deliberate on making the right choice. When this happens, no matter what they end up choosing, they always tend to wonder or wish they had chosen the other option. We can help them to improve their decision-making skills by encouraging them to instinctively follow their own gut instincts and reactions, and follow their first choices. Whether that's choosing what dessert to eat, or the right way to spell a word in a spelling test. Our children won't go far wrong when they learn to trust themselves and take decisive action. In most cases, they do actually know the right answer or decision to make for them. All they have to do is learn how to trust themselves to be happy with their decisions. Asking them what they think **they** should do and being supportive of their decisions builds confidence. Allowing them to make little decisions now, prepares them for those bigger decisions they will one day have to make when we won't always be around to decide what's best for them. Decisiveness plays a huge factor in success, and it's something our children should not fear. They won't always make the right decisions, but that's okay, because mistakes and failures can be their best teachers in life.

FAILURE—OUR CHILDREN'S BEST TEACHER

It's easy to get upset, angry, and frustrated whenever our children make mistakes, but we shouldn't punish them for their mistakes, they are a part of learning not to be denied, hidden, or viewed as negative. No one's perfect, everyone makes them, but it's how we deal with our children's mistakes and how they learn to cope with them that counts. We teach them about mistakes and failure by how we react and respond to our children when they make them. We show them how to overcome them by openly admitting to our children whenever we are wrong or have made a mistake and by apologizing and taking positive steps to make things right. They learn far more from us admitting to our mistakes than they do by us lying to them. When we are honest, we teach them, it's okay to make a mistake, as long as we learn from them.

Lack of experience and immaturity means they have to learn the hard way through mistakes and failure, but how we respond is our responsibility.

Mistakes and failures are not such a bad thing for our children to encounter, yes, they will encounter less failures and make fewer mistakes now if given fewer decisions to make. Having more choices and practicing being decisive while young will obviously bring those failures and mistakes to them a lot quicker than if they allowed others to decide for them. Still, it's better to learn through mistakes while young, than keep making them throughout their lifetime. Adults are less forgiving of other adults making mistakes!

FAILING FUNNY

If children can learn to learn from mistakes, they can serve a positive, beneficial purpose. Yet we try to protect them from making any. We don't want to see our children hurt, upset, angry, or embarrassed, but they need to learn how to deal with those inevitable emotions. Often, we project how we feel when we make a mistake onto them, but children are not so afraid of making mistakes, they are less socially aware of others, making them feel less ashamed and embarrassed by mistakes than we are. If they were more aware, they wouldn't want to try anything new through fear of failure. That's why most adults fail to reach their true potential in life— through fear of looking silly or of doing something wrong in front of others. Most young children find looking silly or doing something wrong funny.

One day, at my son's School Assembly, a young boy accidently fell off the stage at a very apt moment. Instead of feeling embarrassed, the boy got up laughing, and all the other children on stage, and parents in the audience, followed, it was such a comical moment that it made the whole show. I doubt a grown up would have taken it so well. Next time our children make a mistake, we need to become aware of how we respond to them and reflect on why their mistakes and failures make us feel a certain way.

Every mistake or failure gives them the opportunity to learn and grow. Often, they won't know why or how they made a mistake, so the best approach is to be subtle with any corrections, offering them an alternative way to do something next time. It can be tempting to point out mistakes if we feel we are teaching our children right from wrong, but it's how we do that that's important.

If they point to a man and say 'She's up a ladder,' instead of saying 'That's not a woman that's a man,' We could correct their error by saying, 'Yes, *he's* up the ladder.' By emphasizing the he's, we are teaching them the right way without telling them that they are wrong.

FAILURE IS ALWAYS AN OPTION

Children only fail if they fail to try. Highlighting their successes should be our main focus. One wee on the potty is better than none at all, they haven't failed because they had an accident while toilet training, they've succeeded at least once by trying. They will learn their most memorable lessons through failure, and these will be the lessons they will tend to not want to repeat again. Allowing them to fail can be difficult, failure is deemed far from being successful, but they learn how to overcome obstacles and challenges when we let them face and deal with them. They will always learn more from doing than being told, so wrapping them up in cotton wool won't help them. If they aren't failing or making some mistakes, then it's a fair bet they aren't learning anything new or stretching them enough, learning is about trial and error.

OVERCOMING FEAR OF FAILURE

When we approve of them, and they feel they are supported, we remove the greatest obstacle from their path; fear of failure. When it comes to reaching their goals, they need to understand there's a fine line between fear and excitement, fear can feel like excitement, and excitement can feel like fear. One will propel them forward, and the other will hold them back. When they learn to channel that fear and use that energy to attain the outcome they most want, they will be able to turn fear and failure into success. When nervous over sitting a test at school, we can remind them of that feeling of excitement they once had at landing a role in the school play and how they felt a little stage fright before they went on to perform, but once on stage, that all dissolved when everyone cheered them on. And once they have passed their test in school, their fear will turn into a happy feeling of accomplishment. If they feel fear, anxiety, shy, or nervous, we don't want to let them think that whatever they have to face is something to be afraid of, it's far better in the long run to gently encourage them to confront whatever person or situation that is making them feel that way immediately. Those feelings will only persist and get worse if they try to delay or avoid it.

APPRECIATING FAILURE

Appreciating mistakes and failures for the awareness they bring, regardless how uncomfortable the emotions they evoke may be, is part of progress. They offer a chance to grow and learn. That will make children stronger and more self-aware and confident. They won't get to the top by clinging on tightly to the bottom through fear of falling down. When they do brave it and fall down, we can pick them back up again by pointing out to them all the good in their lives, reminding them of all the things that they have already achieved that would not have been possible had they not tried in the first place and risked failing. Also, by reminding them of all the friends and family they have who love them no matter whether they succeed or not. Acknowledging and appreciating what they already have stops them obsessing over their failures and what they don't have or have not yet achieved. There will always be a better way to do a thing, or someone else who has achieved more, but if they focus on that, they will miss what they have achieved or fail to celebrate the success they have already attained. Failure is the stepping stone to success, not the barrier. They need to get into the habit of feeling comfortable with being uncomfortable and appreciate the lessons failure teaches. Once they are on good terms with it, any fear about failure or doing the wrong thing will cease to exist as they realise they can learn from everything and that no experience is ever wasted and nothing is either right or wrong, just different ways of doing or seeing things, all with equal value.

RESILIENCE

When they see the beauty in every experience, including the challenging ones, they stop beating themselves up. It's not failure or what goes wrong that's the problem, it is how our children deal with it and how good they are at being able to pick themselves back up again and carry on. Our attitude will determine how quickly they bounce back from problems, if they feel like a failure, then they will adopt a defeatist attitude. Likewise, the amount of empathy we have toward them in times of trouble will determine the amount of compassion they have for themselves. We need to reassure them that they did what they could do the best they could at that time, and that's always good enough. Encourage them to practice treating themselves with the same level of love and understanding they would to their best friend who was in the same situation.

They need to build inner strength and have faith to keep going. We can be that beacon of hope and light in a dark place that can reach out and help them to get back up and carry on regardless of setbacks, failures, or obstacles along the way. But at times, we have to stand back while they make their own mistakes, waiting in the wing to pick them back up and dust them off when they do. They will always meet challenges, but we can be there by listening, reassuring, and assisting them.

BUILDING RESILIENCE THROUGH COPING MECHANISMS

We can instil in our children the motto; 'Winners never quit and quitters never win' to get them through when times are tough.

They will have to learn ways to support themselves and building their own defence mechanisms and resilience is something our children will have to learn to do for themselves as well. We can 'kiss the baddy cut better' but we can't always take the pain or scarring away. No loving parent would ever want their child to experience pain or heartache, but over protecting or hiding difficulties away from them only limits their ability to learn how to cope with difficulty and limits their capacity to build up resilience. Divorce or bereavements can have devastating effects on young children when they are not addressed appropriately, but being able to face challenging situations helps our children to better understand what is going on, and shows them that they do have the strength and support to get through it. Having experienced difficulties and survived, they will know they can deal and cope with anything in the future the same way. If all they have in their life is us or schoolwork, then if something should happen, like we find a new partner or if they struggle at school, they will be left with a big void in their life. Leading a full life with lots of hobbies, past times, friends, family, sporting interests, a club, or church means, if one is missing, there's plenty of other things to keep them going and will aid in their resilience if things go wrong in one area. It's the support from a strong network that enables them to overcome adversity or difficulties. Most can get over their best friend moving away if they have lots of other friends to support them, it's this counter balancing that helps them to survive and thrive. However, there's only so many knock backs and upset any one person can take, especially if they come together or one after another, so counterbalancing bad experiences with positive ones is vital. Making time for Us Time, doing something fun, is essential in the middle of a crisis or upset. We may not feel like it if something serious or sad is going on, but this is exactly the time our children need a positive distraction the most.

RESILIENCE

Children's resilience can be battered by unpredictability in their daily lives. Parents working together as one team and having routines in place to support them helps build resilience. Our children can easily bounce back from minor disruptions when they know we love them, and they have the security of a robust, consistent routine to fall back on.

We can't hide our children from the unwanted events in the world, but we help them build resilience by allowing them to take responsibility for themselves, make mistakes they can learn from, form relationships with peers that can provoke emotions, and by us not glossing over issues. Resilience is a state of mind children adopt.

SQUEEZING EVERY DROP OF JUICE OUT OF LIFE

We have all heard the question 'are you a glass half empty or full type of person?'

Half full is always better than completely empty, but most tend to focus on the half that's empty. Especially children, have you ever poured a drink for more than one child and witnessed them arguing over who had the most juice in their cup?

If so, you've probably seen one child pouring from one cup into the other to even them up, making sure one doesn't get a drop more than the other.

No child likes to think that the other child has had more than they have had. Siblings are constantly squabbling for attention and more than what the other has. This comes from a not enough for everyone belief and a glass half empty view. If we scold them for being silly, we confirm this belief of 'Yes, I've been hard done by and no one cares I've got less, next time, I'm going to be the one who has the most juice!'

But this is an ideal opportunity to teach them that there's more than enough for everyone.

Overlooking what's good or what they have in favour of what's not so good or what they don't have is an outlook they will automatically adopt if we let them. This following scenario gives us an insight to the thought processes our children have. Let's say Lucy has had a lovely morning playing with her friend Sally. They've role played and dressed up and done puzzles, laughing together in the garden. Snack time arrives, and Lucy becomes upset that Sally has more juice in her cup than she does. Suddenly, the sunny, fun morning turns grey and cloudy, interspersed by Lucy's tears. Lucy's Mum arrives to pick her up from Sally's house and asks 'Did you have fun?'

All Lucy can see is the negative part of the morning as she replies 'No, Sally had more juice than I did!' She has completely overlooked all the fun she has had with her friend and focuses only on what she believes to be important—her lack, and that's the memory she will take from that situation if she is allowed to.

Children don't rationalise. It's black or its white in their mind, grey does not exist. Even though Sally's Mum poured the juice, not Sally, Lucy may blame Sally and say, 'I'm not your friend anymore.'

As Sally or Lucy's parents, what would you think about this situation? Write any thoughts down on how you think you would react as either parent.

If like most parents, you probably wouldn't normally give it much thought, as children squabble all the time. But we can clearly see Sally's intentions were good, and she's been kind to Lucy, inviting her over to play at her house with her, and they've had lots of fun. Yet, Sally now feels confused and upset by Lucy's reaction. Sally may think, 'I'm not inviting friends over to play again, as we will fall out.' Sally then blames herself as she predicts what may happen if she invites anyone else over. As far as we know, Sally's not clairvoyant.

She is however, trying to make sense of the situation and put what she has learnt from her experience together to help her avoid this unwelcome situation reoccurring in the future. This is how we all learn, and this learning while young builds a child's core belief system that may stay with them even when they become adults if no one questions their beliefs.

If Sally can be reassured that this was a one off incident, and that her other friend Lily has come over to play lots of times and they've never fallen out, so this was obviously more to do with how Lucy was feeling than anything Sally had done, Sally may feel reassured enough to invite another friend over next time or even invite Lucy over again to make friends, helping her to remember how much fun they have together. This explanation and reassurance help's Sally to build her resilience up. Falling out with friends will undoubtedly happen again in the future, as this is what children do, but by facing and overcoming that fear, it becomes easier to deal with and accept.

Now, all young children think like Lucy, she wasn't just a spoilt child who wanted her own way. It's natural for a young child to think this way, but this is a chance for us to teach Lucy there is another way to look at the cup. If we don't correct Lucy's assumptions that she didn't have fun just because it seemed like she had less juice, Lucy will automatically only ever notice the negatives, and these will always outweigh any positives.

If we can remind Lucy of all the fun she had with her friend Sally that morning, she can see her cup as it really is—half full not empty.

It's important our children get a balanced view of situations; this is not merely just thinking 'positive' (although I firmly believe we will always achieve more and feel better thinking positively than negatively), but it's about considering the bigger picture. i.e. the fun time Lucy had with Sally dressing up and doing puzzles. When we only see half the picture, that's when we focus on the missing juice in the cup.

Self-Healing

As already mentioned, being open and honest with our children is best, children aren't dumb, they usually know what's going on, so pretending everything is okay when it isn't doesn't equip our children to deal with these issues. Sometimes, leaving a wound to breathe, rather than smothering it with cotton wool or a band aid, is the quickest way to heal itself.

Children just want to understand, and it's this understanding on life that helps give them a sense of involvement and control over their own lives.

When children are allowed to learn for themselves and make mistakes, they feel secure we are there to help if they need us, and not just there to judge, criticize, or tell them off. This helps our children to embrace challenges with an air of confidence in their ability to deal with issues that arise, instead of feeling powerlessly frozen with fear and insecurity.

Children are resilient, but every child is unique and will display varying degrees of resilience. How we as parents build the foundation for them to grow and develop, such as the rules and routines we provide, will determine the level of resilience they have. But exposure is a part of growing up and learning how to heal and overcome. Once children learn to self-heal, the world of opportunity opens up. They are not afraid to venture out into the world and risk a life full of joy, happiness, and love through fear of getting hurt, abandoned, or judged. Then their heart and head are open to whatever comes, knowing they can deal with it no matter what.

The only lesson any of us need to take away to be confident parents and for our children to become happy, healthy, and successful is that we are all constantly learning. Languid learning lasts, so go easy on yourself as you would your little child while learning anything new. Our children are our biggest teachers always, what we glean over the years will come from our experiences and mistakes we made with them. Take time to appreciate those 'aha' moments along the way, and remember, your child is a gift, enjoy the present!

FINAL WORD

PARENTING REQUIRES AN INFINITE amount of patience. In the beginning, implementing any new routine will require patience, energy, and understanding on everyone's part. The secret to successful routines depends on how patient we are at carrying them out and how we encourage our children to follow them.

It means showing unconditional love, even when they go against their routines and not rushing them.

Start by introducing one new routine at a time and start as you mean to go on (remember our motto?).

Each child and circumstance are different, but most, if not all, children will get used to routines so don't worry.

The whole point of routine is to help our children, not to punish them in any way. Sometimes, it may take a while for them to understand that routines are for their own good though. It's at that time we will encounter challenging behaviour. They are not trying to test us and parenting is not a test, although at times, it's certainly very testing. None of us will have to sit an exam at the end of it or prove anything to anyone.

I believe that every parent in life does the very best that they can with the knowledge and circumstances that they find themselves in. And that is always good enough, you need not prove anything to anyone but yourself.

The only people we need to please are ourselves and our children, and that's a moment by moment effort.

None of us are bad parents because we lose it from time to time. We are just normal people, coping with the normal trials and tribulations of parenting. The issues we encounter with our children are timeless classics that will never go out of fashion. Although we deal with them differently over the years, they are one and the same problems our own parents encountered with us, and our grandparents with our parents.

Take comfort in the fact that times change, but parenting dilemmas remain. All we can do is stay strong and be confident in the fact that we are all doing the best that we can at any given time, and that is always good enough.

WHAT IF MY CHILD REGRESSES OR REFUSES TO FOLLOW THE U URSELF ROUTINE?

Don't panic, it's perfectly normal for children to resist routine and to flex their authority from time to time. In fact, I would be more worried if they passively didn't. After all, we don't want perfect children, we want happy, healthy, successful children, and having their own mind is a good sign of a healthy, happy, and successful child.

As long as we remain confident and consistent, and do not give in to their rebellion no matter what, then eventually, they will see that we mean business. When they realise that that's the way it's going to be from now on, they will learn acceptance

Once they come to understand, and believe me over time they will, that what you are trying to achieve is all for their own good, then they will happily adjust and start rebelling over another issue instead.

These parenting challenges that our children throw at us never stops, we've still got the teens to go through... there are different phases around every corner to look forward too.

The best and really only thing we can do is stay confident in the face of our children. You may not love them for their insolence at times, but they will love you for your strength.

Having read this far, you can safely say that you are obviously a very loving parent. Not perfect, because there simply is no perfect parent, and there is no perfect child, they do not exist.

But what you hopefully now realise is that you are the perfect parent for your child, and that your child is perfectly themselves. No one else could ever take the place of you or your child. Even a second, third, fourth or more child will have their own unique place in your heart that cannot be replaced or replicated by another.

The bond you share with each child, regardless of what condition it is in today, is a unique bond. It is a beautiful, intrinsically binding of love that ties you together, long after the umbilical cord has been cut.

Ultimately, how you parent your child is up to you, but you are not alone on your parenting journey. You already have the best teacher that you could ever need guiding you and offering you valuable lessons along the way—your child!

In my life, I have been blessed to care for and to be loved and taught by so many children throughout my career of working with children, but the ones who have taught me the best lessons of love, patience, compassion, and understanding are my own two beautiful, happy, healthy, and successful children, Holly and Dylan. Both of whom I am most proud of and eternally grateful to. Without them, this book would never have been written.

IT'S NEVER TOO LATE

It's never too late to be a confident parent and raise happy, healthy, and successful children. You can start today, now, this very minute and from where you are with the knowledge that you now have to make the appropriate changes that need to be made in your child's life.

However they arrived in your life, planned for, unexpected, adopted, or fostered, they are all individuals in their own right. Perfect in every way, with limitless capabilities and infinite possibilities ahead of them. Ready and waiting for you to unwrap their layers and discover who they are and who they can become with your love and support.

Every day from now on, choose only to dwell on your child's uniqueness. Love and appreciate them for the person they are. Guide and support them through their childhood journey of discovery, or through their adulthood, because it's never too late to be there for them. Be in awe of them every step of the way, noticing how they really are awesome.

The health, happiness, and success of our children is not determined by education, opportunities, or even by genetics alone. It can be nurtured by us as parents by how we live and love moment by moment, day by day.

How good we feel and how good our children feel about themselves as a result, is the real success of parenting and the true measure of our children's health, happiness, and success in life. And it is something that we can influence and change for better or for worse at any time we choose to.

No matter how we choose to spend our time with our children, we should endeavour to make it an enjoyable experience, one that reflects our unconditional love, or what is the point?

One way or another, we chose to have our children in our lives, they were powerless to that decision. Therefore, surely, it's our responsibility to make sure that they enjoy their time with us and on this earth and that we appreciate the unique gift of life that we have been given.

As individual parents, we can't eliminate all the wars, crime, poverty, or despair in the world, but we can change ourselves and guide our children along a different path. If our children are not part of the problem, then they will always be part of the solution. One by one, we all make a difference. Collectively as parents lovingly raising happy, healthy, and successful children, we gradually shape a different future for all of mankind.

From now on, if we can choose only to dwell on our children's uniqueness and love and appreciate them for the person they are, we will be in a better position to guide and support them through their childhood journey of discovery. Even if you have only recently reconnected with your child for whatever reason or have just met them for the first time, as in the case of foster care or adoption, then it's never too late to be a warm, confident, proactive, and present parent.

All any new routine ever really needs is time. Time is priceless, but so are our children.

ENJOY THE PROCESS AND GET IN TOUCH!

PARENTING IS A VERY rewarding time and can be lots of fun if we let it. Enjoy and treat every day as a special one, because while your child is young, every day really is special and full of firsts. First words, first steps, first pee on the potty, first day at school, first boyfriend, all of which are magical moments for you and your child to cherish.

Believe me, the time really does go so quickly, one day you are crying into your pillow, begging for some sleep while they are teething, the next you are crying into a tissue as you are waving them off to university!

If nothing else, I hope this book has helped you to become more confident as a parent and to enjoy the parenting journey as much as your child enjoys being your child.

This book's intention throughout was focused on solutions to everyday parenting problems. I hope it has helped you, if so, I would love to hear all about it and how your child has got on with the U URSELF Routine either by leaving me a review on Amazon or via social media. If you would like to email me personally with an issue, you can email me at emma@happychildcare.club I may not always be able to answer every question personally, but I endeavour to cover them in blog posts or future books.

You can also tag or make contact with me through my social media platforms using the following hashtags:

#ConfidentParents
#PowerfulParents
#PresentParenting
#ProactiveParenting
#ProactiveParents

My social media are as follows:

    https://twitter.com/EmmaGrantAuthor
    https://www.facebook.com/1977therapy
    https://emmagrantauthor.com/
    https://www.instagram.com/emgrantauthor
    https://www.happychildcare.club
    https://www.facebook.com/pg/EmmandPaulGrant
    https://www.instagram.com/happychildcarepentwyn

And if you have any issue's managing your child's unwanted behaviour, you may like to join me in my next book, *The Powerful Proactive Parent's Guide to Present Parenting*. Available from Amazon and all good book stockists now.

Love and best wishes,
Em x

GLOSSARY OF TERMS

You may come across some or all of these terms in my series of books. In case you aren't familiar with my books, below is a glossary of the most common phrases or words and what they mean.

Auto Pilot Parents or Parenting: means a parent who is distracted or who responds, reacts, and behaves in a habitual way,] without thinking about what they are doing or why.

Perfect: perfect in the eyes and expectations of others.

Powerful Parents or Power: refers to parents who have influence and can use this influence to positively teach, guide, and coach.

Present Parenting: being Present means being conscious in the moment.

Proactive Parents or Proactive Parenting or a Proactive Approach: the word 'proactive' here means taking action in advance or being involved. It means pre-empting and preventing issues before they occur. Prevention is better than a cure!

The U URSELF Routine: a mnemonic for You Yourself, and stands for a routine that consists of the following:

U Time
Us Time
Recreation
Sleep
Esteem
Love
Food

DISCLAIMER

This is a non-fiction book; therefore, the anecdotes within the book are all true. If they were made-up stories, they would make up a work of fiction, not fact. However, no individuals have been named.

The sole intention of this book is help us to learn from past parenting/childcare professionals and their experiences so we can make positive changes. It is not in any way intended to judge or condemn anyone or the experiences they have encountered or created. All the opinions and beliefs expressed throughout are my own.

Over the years, parents and children have come and gone to and from my setting, yet all the situations and parenting issues remain the same. Therefore, if you can identify with a story, it's probably not you, but if you're like most of us parents, there's a chance it could be, too.

All information is based on my own personal opinions and experiences from my role as a Mum, Registered Childminder, Parent Coach, and Hypnotherapist. Although based on real-life scenarios and facts, I do not claim to heal, diagnose or treat anyone.

All concerns regarding your child whether physical, psychological, or emotional should be addressed by a qualified professional, such as your own GP. I offer recommendations to help you, as a parent, to manage and enjoy the parenting journey based on what I have found has worked over the years with other parents, but I do not claim my way to be the best way for everyone, or indeed to be the only way.

Take from this book what feels right, what suits, and what works best for you, your child and family, and follow your own parental intuition and instincts always.

ACKNOWLEDGEMENTS

Thank you to all the many parents and children I have had the pleasure and privilege to look after and work with over the past sixteen years at Happy Childcare. Without you all, this book would never have been written, so thank you all very much.

Also, special thanks to Hayley Paige, my publisher, and the team at Notebook Publishing (Marni, my editor; and Mark, my cover designer): your support and creativity has been invaluable.

ABOUT THE AUTHOR

Emma L Grant is a Mum, Hypnotherapist, Nutritional Therapist, and Parenting Coach/Counsellor.

She has also been a Registered Childminder for the past sixteen years, with a Level 5 Diploma in Leadership and Management in Children's Care, Learning and Development.

She works alongside her husband, living in Cardiff, UK, with their teenage children.

www.ingramcontent.com/pod-product-compliance
Lightning Source LLC
Chambersburg PA
CBHW072341090426
42741CB00012B/2876